Winning the Retirement Game

A FUNDAMENTAL GAME PLAN
DESIGNED TO SECURE YOUR RETIREMENT BLISS

Jeff Dixson

Northwest Financial & Tax Solutions, Inc.
VANCOUVER, WASHINGTON

Jeff Dixson / Northwest Financial & Tax Solutions, Inc.
12405 SE 2nd Circle, Suite 100
Vancouver, WA 98684
www.nwfts.net

Book Layout ©2013 BookDesignTemplates.com

Ordering Information:
For details, contact the address above.

Winning the Retirement Game / Jeff Dixson. —1st ed.
ISBN 978-1522875215

Contents

To my wife Brenda, my children and my grandkids, who have always motivated me to be the best I can be and have fueled my desire to rise to the top in a very competitive and challenging industry.

Introduction

If you are a baby boomer like me, I would like to ask you a question. Is the world we live in today the same as the one in which we all grew up? Did you just shake your head "no," perhaps even emphatically so? I agree with you. It's a totally different place. And I'm sure you're not just thinking about science and technology either. Attitudes are different. People are different. I can remember a time when folks didn't lock their doors and even left their car keys in the ignition. Think about that. It says something about the mood and spirit of America in the 1950s, doesn't it?

Like many boys who grew up in the '50s and '60s, I worked and played and went to school in an America that was reflected pretty accurately by the shows we watched on our black-and-white television sets. (Let me clarify for younger readers that in those days they were not called TVs. That came later. They were called "television sets" because they were usually a piece of furniture and there was usually one per household, *if you were wealthy* enough to afford one.)

I think there are cable channels these days that run these old shows — "Leave it to Beaver," "Father Knows Best," "Ozzie and Harriet." The plots may be a bit thin and the humor may be a little corny by today's standards, but you can pick up on a sense of innocence and decency the country seemed to possess in more abundance back then. The nation was of a different social fabric in those days. Dad worked while Mom stayed home. The kids may have been mischievous at times, but they weren't disrespectful. Nothing was dark or troubled. A bit too glossy? Maybe. But it wasn't too far off the mark, and it was the way we saw ourselves.

If I had to pick a time when the all of that changed, I would have to say it was about the time in November 1963 when three rifle shots fired from the sixth floor of a warehouse in Dallas, Texas, took the life of John F. Kennedy, the young, vibrant president who seemed so iconically to represent America's bright future.

Our slice of Americana was not quite as prosperous as what we saw depicted on TV back then. We lived in Portland, Oregon, where my father was a postal worker and at times held down two other jobs in order to support me, my mother, my three brothers and my two sisters. My first job, when I was 9 years old, was delivering The Oregonian, Portland's major daily newspaper. Even that has changed. More people are reading their news online. I learned the value of money at an early age. If I wanted new shoes instead of ill-fitting hand-me-downs, I would have to earn the money myself. So I got up at 5 a.m. each day and finished my paper route before school. If it sounds like I'm complaining, I'm not. Looking back, I am glad I had those experiences. I can relate to people from every background because of them. I am even grateful for the privations associated with growing up poor. Our family may have had little in the way of material things, but there was never a shortage of love. I am convinced that deprivation is the soul of appreciation. Doing without taught me appreciation for the good things that have come my way in life.

The first handheld calculator was invented in 1967. How amazing is that? We've come a long way since then; technology has grown by leaps and bounds. In today's day and age, you can wear glasses that are a computer. They can take pictures and videos, send text messages, show directions directly in front of your eyes, and on top of that, this is all done by voice command! The world has also become more complicated in many ways.

Back in 1960, CPR was invented and in 1964, the measles vaccine was created. Today, medicine has advanced to the point where there have been many successful multi-limb transplants. Even more amazing than that, scientists can grow new body parts from your own stem cells! The result of modern medicine and education about nutrition and exercise is people are living longer.

Careers have changed too. It used to be that when you found your job, you worked for that company for 40 years or so. You were loyal to that company and they were loyal to you. They rewarded your years of service with a pension. When you retired, you didn't have to worry too much about your finances; your pension and Social Security were consistent and were always there for you. Retirement was much shorter then, too, lasting perhaps five or 10 years on average.

America has always been about pulling yourself up by your own bootstraps, and that's how retirement is for many. Drastically fewer people have pensions, causing some to bounce around from company to company, seeking to move up the income ladder to compensate. Fifty years ago, no one had heard of such things as 401(k) and 403(b) retirement plans. What was an IRA or an RMD a half century ago? There was no need in the 1950s and 1960s to read retirement books by Suze Orman, Dave Ramsey or Robert T. Kyosaki ("Rich Dad Poor Dad"). Now, retirement lasts longer and, like the world, it has become much more complex. Let me clarify that a bit. To quote a line from "Flash Boys: A Wall Street Revolt" by Michael Lewis: "People think that complex is an advanced state of complicated ... it's not. A car key is simple. A car is complicated. A car in traffic is complex."

Retirement has become a complex state of affairs. Decisions, decisions, decisions. Should I trust the stock market with all of my hard-earned assets or is there a formula that I should follow? Will Social Security be there for the duration of my retirement? Should I claim my benefits as soon as possible? Wait until I am at full retirement age? Wait until I am age 70? Is there any way to reduce my taxes? Do I need to establish a trust? Should I buy long-term care, or LTC, insurance?

Questions like that would fill up two more pages of this book and there would still be more. One of the main reasons I wanted to write this book is to convey, in some permanent and multi-distributable form, some of the things I have learned in life that can serve to help those who are at the crossroads in this new age of retirement. The title of this book, "Winning the Retirement Game," is not meant to convey the idea that retirement is a frivolous exercise or a sport. Not at all! Living as well in retirement as we lived during our working years is not a game that is played for you anymore, but one that you have to play for yourself. And, like a game, there are strategies involved — or at least, there should be — if we are to be successful at it. It is critical to remember that retirement is a marathon, not a sprint.

In many ways, retirement planning reminds me of the strategies involved in coaching youth sports, something I have enjoyed for many years now. The "X's and the O's" we call them when we are getting ready for a game. The same goes for retirement. Where you choose to place your assets prior to and during your retirement can make the difference between living an independent, carefree life and having to depend on others. It can be the difference between having the freedom to fulfill your dreams and worrying about how you are going to make ends meet. Between choosing to thrive in retirement and not just survive.

When should you collect your Social Security so as to get the most out of the program? That is a strategy decision. Strategies can determine whether you overpay your taxes and end up shortchanging either yourself or your loved ones when you — how did Shakespeare put it? "Shuffle off this mortal coil?" But while we are still on this "mortal coil" (whatever that means) we have many decisions to make regarding how we spend, use, distribute, invest and allocate our resources. Those are the decisions I would like to talk to you about in this book.

In my career as a financial professional I have seen far too many people postpone making those decisions until it is too late. They don't exactly plan to fail. They just fail to plan. Some make wrong decisions. Perhaps they were given bad advice from well-meaning but ill-educated friends. Or perhaps they were victims of wrong (wrong for them, anyway) directions from an advisor who had dollar signs for eyes. It could have been that they threw their hands up in frustration at all the conflicting financial advice that seems to clog the media these days and simply decided to become a financial "do-it-yourselfer." Regardless of the reason, the effects are the same if the strategy is not a workable one and the direction taken is the wrong one.

Coaching young people in several sports over the years taught me some basic truths. Winning isn't everything. It's more important for young people playing a sport to have fun. And, yes, kids need to learn to be polite and gracious to their opponents. Having said that, winning surely beats losing every time. As a coach, I try to teach kids the skills, fundamentals and strategies they need to win. Why? Because I have seen the joy and exuberance on their faces when they win, contrasted with the glum, downcast expressions when they lose. I cannot in good conscience tell them that it just doesn't matter. Of course it matters. Everything matters. I am proud of them either way, win or lose. But they can see the happiness for them on my face when the scoreboard declares them victors. In contrast with youth sports, the game of retirement has much more dire consequences if you lose.

The people I have coached to and through retirement know I want them to win, not lose their resources. When the dust began to settle after the 2008 market crash, I had many quiet celebrations over the phone and in my office with clients who were thankful that their retirement nest eggs were still intact. Did the strategies I employed help them win that round with Wall Street? I would like to think so. But I was proud of them too, because they were able to embrace the concepts and fundamentals I had been teaching and make the right decisions.

No, the world is not the same as the one in which we all grew up. So why do so many people still invest their money as if it were?

During the talks I give from time to time on handling finances in retirement, I often compare preparing for retirement to being in what sports writers like to call the "red zone" in a football game — between the 20-yard line and the goal line. It fits because the way the field is marked, the closer you are to the goal line, the more careful you are not to fumble the ball.

On a drive, with the clock running down and the balance of the game depending on whether you put the ball across the goal line, what a shame it would be to have driven the length of the field and have made good decisions right up to, say, the 5-yard line, and then lose the football! It could cost you the game. When you are approaching retirement, you have to be careful not to fumble the ball by making a wrong move that could put all or part of your nonrenewable resources in jeopardy.

Some of the concepts and strategies you will see expressed as you read these pages may be outside your current way of thinking; don't let that throw you. Imagine the college athlete moving to the professional ranks and how foreign to him or her some of the plays and strategies may seem. So, if you see something you haven't seen before, let's explore it together. Check it out, don't check out on it. As you will see, that could be the difference between winning the game of retirement and... well... losing.

CHAPTER 1

It Doesn't Take a Genius

"A danger foreseen is half avoided." ~ Unknown Proverb

Before May 18, 1980, you could stand at some places in Portland and see very clearly off to the northeast the snow covered peak of Mount St. Helens. Back then, it was a peak. It looked like pictures I had seen of Mount Fuji in Japan. All that changed at 8:32 a.m. that Sunday when a lateral explosion caused the north face of the mountain to collapse into a massive avalanche. The blast permanently removed the top of the mountain at an angle, forever ruining its conical symmetry and leaving behind a visibly active volcano. Now, on a clear day, you can still see from our office complex in Vancouver, Washington, what people now refer to as the Mount St. Helens *volcano,* which has become quite a tourist attraction. Approximately 500,000 visitors come every year to watch the smoldering mountain quietly building its lava dome, making peace with the surrounding landscape it so terrorized that spring of 1980.

I was living in Troutdale, Oregon, at the time of the eruption. I remember sitting in my living room, reading the Sunday paper with the TV on, when I heard the news bulletin that the mountain, which had been threatening to blow its top for months, finally had done so. I grabbed my 3-year-old son Jeromy and left Brent, my 9-month-old, with my wife, Brenda, and drove up to the corner of 223rd and Stark Street. As it turned out, the best view of the fuming mountain could be had from the parking lot of Zim's country store. Jeromy and I sat and watched in awe for hours as billows of smoke and ash rose toward the stratosphere. Years later, I would name the two conference rooms in our Vancouver, Washington, office the "Mount Hood Room" and the "Mount St. Helens Room," since both iconic mountains are visible from the property.

Scientists had been reporting signs of increasing instability within the mountain, so it was not a matter of if; it was a matter of when the mountain would explode. In fact, Mount St. Helens had been visibly active for more than 100 years. Scientists knew it was a powder keg and predicted an eruption sometime before the year 2000. On March 16, 1980, a series of small earthquakes occurred in the Cascades. Besides geologists, few people noticed. But then, on the afternoon of March 20, 1980, a magnitude 4.2 earthquake rattled buildings across the state and got everyone's attention. Geologists who got close enough could feel a continuous shaking called "volcano tremor." Steam was coming out of the top of the mountain.

Fifty-seven people were killed during the eruption on May 18, 1980. One was a 30-year-old scientist, David A. Johnston, who studied volcanoes and was fascinated by Mount St. Helens. His obsession cost him his life. Seconds before his campsite was hit by the shockwave of the explosion, Johnson clicked the button on his radio and spoke what were to be his last words: "Vancouver! Vancouver! This is it!" Searchers never found his body. The fact that the eruption occurred on a Sunday was fortunate and probably saved hundreds of lives. Had it occurred during the work week, loggers would have been active in the path of either the blast or the resultant lava and mud flow.

The volcano also claimed the life of an 83-year-old West Virginia native and World War I veteran who had lived near the base of the mountain for 54 years. Once word spread that Mount St. Helens was unstable, local authorities begged the recalcitrant Harry R. Truman to leave but he stubbornly refused, saying at one point, "If the mountain goes, I go with it." His body was never found and is presumed to have been swept away by the wall of mud and debris that overtook his lodge.

More than three decades have passed now, and Mount St. Helens and the 150 square miles that it made into a moonscape are still recovering. Nature is slowly but surely reclaiming the land. Elk can be seen grazing in the meadows just outside the perimeter of the "scorch zone," and here and there flowering plants are growing on the side of the mountain itself.

The Stock Market Crash of 2008

The stock market crash of 2008 was similar to Mount St. Helens in several respects:

- There were warnings signs that went ignored.
- The ones who were hurt were those who took too much risk in the market.
- As this is written, many are still recovering from it.

What caused Mount St. Helens to erupt was pressure building up from inside the earth over a long period of time. The 2008 crash was the result of economic pressure that also built up over time and needed a catalyst, or economic event, to release that pressure in the form of the worst Wall Street disaster since the Great Depression.

Those who were in the housing industry could not have asked for a better economy than the one that existed during the years 2001-2007. You could drive along the fringes of any metropolitan area during that time and hear the syncopated beat of construction hammers nailing up the trusses for new houses as fast as the contractors could lay out the neighborhoods. Everyone involved in the process benefitted, from the lumber truck driver down to the real estate agent. Banks and mortgage companies were certainly enjoying the ride. Money was flowing like a mountain river in springtime. If you had a pulse and could fog a mirror, you could get a loan. Property values were soaring. Buyers were in a race to get their down payments on the books so they could ink the papers to what, in everyone's mind at the time, would forever be going up in value.

With the low interest rates, it just made sense to get in while the getting was good. Don't have enough for the down payment? "No problem," said the mortgage brokers. "We'll put you in a 'piggy-back loan.'" That was the term used for obtaining an instant second mortgage on the home for the down payment along with the first mortgage for the actual monthly payments.

You say you have only been on the job for three months and you have no idea how you are going to make the payments? No problem! You qualify for a No Doc NINA, which stood for a "no documentation, no income, no asset" loan. Still can't afford the payments? We will give you an adjustable rate mortgage. Low payments now that will get higher later. But who cares? Statistics say that people don't live in their houses longer than five years, anyway. One creative lending package that was in vogue at the time was "interest only" loans. You never paid on the principal… just the interest every month.

Can you see the problem that was beginning to develop here?

According to a report released Oct. 20, 2007 by the The Economist magazine, the price of the typical American house increased by 124 percent between 1997 and 2006 with homes selling for almost five times the median household income. By September 2008 home values dropped precipitously, borrowers couldn't make their payments and those with adjustable-rate mortgages couldn't refinance. That's when the defaults began. The chickens hadn't come home to roost just yet, but they certainly were in a landing pattern.

Big Banks Begin to Fail

The definition of "too big to fail" is the idea that a business has become so large and so deeply ingrained in the fabric of the national economy that the government will have to intervene and prevent it from going under. I had never heard the term until U.S. Rep. Stewart McKinney made it popular in 1984 at a congressional hearing discussing the Federal Deposit Insurance Corporation's (FDIC) intervention with Continental Illinois National Bank. Continental was the largest bank failure in history up until 2008 when Washington Mutual went under.

In 2006, few knew or seemed to care what the mega investment banks, like Lehman Brothers, Bear Stearns, Goldman Sachs and Morgan Stanley — all banks that were considered "too big to fail" — were doing. But they were wading deeper and deeper into the tar pit, infecting their financial foundations, perilously weakened by the loose lending practices that had fueled the housing boom. Bear Stearns, the smallest of the "too big" banks, was the first to go. In March 2008, its near insolvency exposed just how shakily these lords of finance were perched atop mountains of bad debt. Bear Stearns, the "old reliable" of the banking industry, known for making good business decisions for more than 80 years, spiraled from sound to nearly bankrupt in just 72 hours and had to be fire sold to J.P. Morgan Chase. By October, several major financial institutions had either failed outright, were acquired under duress, or were subject to government takeover.

Those were days when we began to expect bad news every day. Every morning when we turned on CNN or picked up the newspaper, we learned about yet another government bailout. The list of venerable firms that had to be rescued from the brink included such time-honored firms as Lehman Brothers, Merrill Lynch, Fannie Mae, Freddie Mac, Washington Mutual, Wachovia, Citigroup and AIG.

As a financial advisor specializing in retirement income planning, I saw firsthand the personal toll the 2008 crash took. Some retirees lost as much as half their life savings. Because of the lower-risk focus my firm takes, few of our clients lost significantly. But I heard the horror stories.

In the fall of 2008, as I was preparing to speak at a retirement planning workshop, I could tell as the audience filed in and took their seats that the mood seemed serious and somber. Three days earlier, we had learned that Lehman Brothers had declared bankruptcy and the Dow Jones Industrial Average (DJIA) had dropped 500 points. The following day, the Federal Reserve had announced that it was bailing out the American International Group (AIG) with an $85 billion loan. The day before the meeting, the Dow had fallen another 450 points. Our scheduled topic was "The Most Common Mistakes Retirees Make with Their Finances." But I knew within five minutes that these people were hurting and needed answers. I scrapped my outline and just opened it up to questions.

"Why didn't anyone see this coming?"

"How long will it take for the markets to recover?"

"Why didn't our broker warn us this was coming?"

"What should we do now?"

I felt like a first responder at a crash site. Whose wounds do I treat first? I would later meet with many of them personally and offer solutions and explain investment alternatives that would prevent them from experiencing a similar disaster in the future. But I had to tell them that I had no crystal ball. The problem is many of them were influenced by counselors that acted as if they did have a crystal ball. For some, who had immediate plans for retirement, their plans had to be put on hold while they continued to work to replace what they had lost. Some of those people felt betrayed, and I couldn't blame them.

"Our broker took a week to return our calls," said one man. "And when he did, he told my wife and me that we are 'all in the same boat' and just to hang in there... it will bounce back."

I thought about that after the couple left our office. The broker was right, in a way. Markets do rebound. But it may take decades to recover losses such as the ones these people had experienced. That couple didn't have too many decades in front of them.

Another couple said they had more than $700,000 before the "roof caved in." They had, on the advice of their broker, placed it in a mixture of stocks, bonds, mutual funds and variable annuities. The man said that he had checked his statement online just before coming in for the appointment and his retirement nest egg had shrunk to a little over $480,000.

"That would have sounded like a lot of money to me in my 30s," he said. "But my wife and I own and run a small business, and we had planned on selling it to our oldest son and living off our Social Security and the interest from our savings."

Those dreams were now shattered. They would have to work at least another five years to rebuild.

Anything Can Happen

The bottom line is that anything can happen at any time. The investment world in which we live today is volatile and the stock market is an unpredictable place. In fact, the only thing we can predict about the future is its unpredictability. But there is no reason why we can't be as prepared for the future as possible. Since financial disasters can hit unannounced, getting your assets to a position where they can *grow with safety* is just the prudent thing to do. In succeeding chapters, we will cover some of the ways we should be changing the methods we use to manage the wealth we have accumulated. In financial management, as it is in sports, it starts with the fundamentals: discipline, staying on defense and being willing to commit to a winning game plan.

CHAPTER 2

Hey, What's Going on Here?

"You shall know the truth and the truth shall make you mad." ~ Aldous Huxley

Ⅰf you happen to be strolling along Sixth Avenue in New York City and look up at the façade of the Bank of America Tower, you will see a billboard-sized National Debt Clock. The dot-matrix numbers are racing like a digital speedometer on a rocket ship, telling any who are interested exactly what the United States gross national debt amounts to second by second. The numbers on the right flash so quickly that they are just a blur, so I can't tell you the exact number here. It doesn't matter, anyway. By the time I typed the amount, it would change. Suffice it to say that Uncle Sam is, at the time of this writing, more than $18 trillion in debt.

Because million, billion and trillion all rhyme, it is easy for the difference between these numerical designations to zip right over our heads. Just for review, a million is a thousand thousands. A billion is a thousand million. A trillion is a thousand billion. If that is still a bit abstract, let's illustrate the three "illions" in a way we can all remember.

Million - One million seconds is about 11.5 days. A stack of a million pennies would be about a mile high. One million ants would weigh a little over 6 pounds. If you divided $1 million evenly among the U.S. population, everyone in the country would receive approximately one-third of 1 cent.

Billion - One billion seconds is about 31.5 years. One billion pennies stacked on top of each other would be 870 miles high. If you earn $45,000 a year, it would take 22,000 years to accumulate $1 billion. A billion ants would weigh approximately 3 tons — or about as much as an elephant. If you were to divide $1 billion evenly among the U.S. population, everyone in the country would receive approximately $3.33.

Trillion - One trillion seconds is more than 31,000 years. A stack of 1 trillion pennies would make a tower 870,000 miles high. One trillion pennies would reach to the moon, back to Earth, and back to the moon again. One trillion ants would weigh about 3,000 tons. One trillion dollars divided evenly among the U.S. population pounds would mean that everyone in the country would receive $3,000.[1]

That puts it in perspective, doesn't it? The National Debt Clock has an interesting history. It was the brainchild of New York real estate magnate Seymour Durst. He wanted to call attention to the soaring national debt in 1989 when it was less than $3 trillion. He died in 1995. I wonder what he would have to say today. The clock was actually turned off for a brief period in 2000 when the prosperity of the 1990s resulted in the national debt actually decreasing. That didn't last, however, and the clock was reactivated in July 2002 and has been running like an odometer on steroids ever since. When the debt exceeded $10 trillion in September 2008, another digit had to be added and the original clock was replaced with the one we see today.

---

[1] Courtney Taylor. About.com. "Millions, Billions and Trillions." http://statistics.about.com/od/Applications/a/ Millions-Billions-And-Trillions.htm.

If you don't want to travel to New York City to see the national debt race along, you can visit www.usdebtclock.org on the Web. This website's version of the "clock" displays a running tally of just about every measurable item in the nation's financial universe — everything from how much mortgage debt exists in the country to how many people are currently receiving food stamps. Just how accurate these "clocks" are is up for some debate. Several of them are in operation now, and none of them agree in synchronicity. But they are all close.

What these "clocks" display is scary on many levels. It's not just the federal government that's awash in this debt. Every man, woman and child currently alive and even those of future generations in the United States are and will be affected by this red-ink tsunami. We are robbing Peter to pay Paul. Our appetite for goods and services is writing checks our gross domestic product can't cash. If the United States was a corporation, it would be bankrupt.

David Walker, comptroller general of the United States from 1998 to 2008, in 2009 compared the country's financial situation to a fiscal cancer. As far back as 2006, it was publicly recognized that the underpinnings of our financial house were becoming unstable. A USA Today article by Dennis Cauchon dated Aug. 4, 2006, when the national debt was flirting with only $3 trillion, stated: "The federal government keeps two sets of books. The set the government doesn't talk about is the audited financial statement produced by the government's accountants following standard accounting rules."

The article went on to say that if Social Security and Medicare were included in the accounting, as would be called for under standard accounting rules, the deficit would be much greater.

"Congress has written its own accounting rules — which would be illegal for a corporation to use because they ignore important costs such as the growing expense of retirement benefits for civil servants and military personnel," the article explained.

When the federal government promises $100 million worth of aid and subsidies, they only account for what comes out of the Treasury — regardless of how much they promised to pay and regardless of the time frame in which they promised to pay it. When we evaluate the national debt using standard accounting principles, the deficit would amount to a far, far higher number — upwards of $87 trillion at this writing in October 2015. That's approximately $245,000 for every man, woman and child in the United States! This debt is going to affect your retirement and the retirement of future generations.

Let's turn our attention to Social Security, one of the solid pillars that most retirees and people thinking about retirement rely on. Consider this: Social Security statements issued in 2013 contained the following ominous message on the front page under the heading "About Social Security's Future." Keep in mind, these are not my words, they are the words of the Social Security Administration, and they are printed in rather large print, there for all to see:

"Social Security is a compact between generations. Since 1935, America has kept the promise of security for its workers and their families. Now, however, the Social Security system is facing serious financial problems, and action is needed soon to make sure the system will be sound when today's younger workers are ready for retirement.

"Without changes, in 2033 the Social Security Trust Fund will be able to pay only about 77 cents for each dollar of scheduled benefits.* We need to resolve these issues soon to make sure Social Security continues to provide a foundation of protection for future generations."

" *These estimates are based on the intermediate assumptions from the Social Security Trustees' Annual Report to the Congress."

Pretty sobering, eh? Clearly this system is broken. As this is written, the United States is racking up debt like there's no tomorrow and the Social Security Administration statement makes it very clear there simply will not be enough money in the Social Security sys-

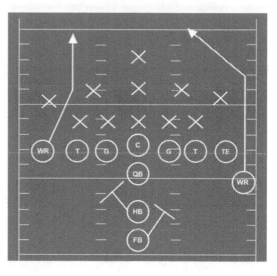

tem for future generations to rely on for consistent retirement income. That is, unless the problem is fixed. To fix the problem, there are essentially three things the SSA and United States government can do.

- Spend less
- Tax more
- Continue to devalue the dollar

Economic experts agree that the U.S. is such a big player in the world economy that to continue to devalue the dollar would soon create a global economic crisis. As I write this in October 2015, the Federal Reserve is spending $85 billion a month in an effort to keep inflation down. Clearly, deflation or devaluing the dollar isn't on the government's agenda. To spend less would seem to be the most attractive of the two remaining choices, but I do not see lawmakers moving in that direction. That leaves *tax more.*

If that turns out to be true, and the United States government does decide to put the burden on the American people to recover the floundering system, what impact might that have on your retirement? Here's something to think about: The argument for tax-deferred savings plans has always been that you should build up your account while you're working, while you are in a *higher* tax bracket, and tap into it when your income falls, at which time you will ostensibly be in a *lower* tax bracket. Have you heard that one? There's only one hitch to that way of thinking. We don't *know* what taxes will be in the future, do we? With the national debt clock rolling up trillions of dollars in future obligations, all indications are that taxes will be higher, not lower, in the future. One solution to this tax increase is to invest in a Roth IRA. You fund the Roth with taxed dollars, which means you won't get a tax deduction when you contribute to the account. But your distributions will be completely tax-free after you've had the account for five years and after you reach age 59 ½. The choice between tax deferral like a 401(k), 403(b), or traditional IRA and a Roth IRA is a strategy decision. The traditional IRA is a "taxed forever" account. The Roth IRA is a "taxed never" account once taxes are paid on the initial principal (if withdrawn after five years or after age 59 ½). Roth IRA conversions — paying taxes on the *seed,* not the *harvest!*

Politicians seem to run with the tax ball when they are campaigning and then reverse field after they are elected. I call it the "read my lips" syndrome. "If I'm elected I won't raise your taxes," was a more recent claim. "I'm going to raise the taxes on the top 1 or 2 percent." What actually happened, of course, was that every taxpayer in the country had their taxes raised — just not in a way they could see it. When we see that the *government* was bailing out the banks, and the *government* was bailing out the auto industry, it's easy to lose sight of the fact that *taxpayers* of the government are the ones who are doing the bailing, and it's our elected government officials who are deciding how our tax dollars are being spent. If they spend badly, it's fully within their power to make us pay more in taxes. In early 2014, the U.S. House of Representatives passed a bill authorizing another $1.1 trillion spending plan. Has irresponsible spending with borrowed money become a habit so ingrained with lawmakers that they can't help themselves? Can such spending really lead elsewhere but higher taxes and higher interest rates down the road? It may even be that our children and grandchildren — the nation's young people of today — will inherit the bill for our current spending in some form. Many suspect that the Social Security income older Americans receive will not be there in its present form for younger Americans.

With pensions becoming increasingly rare, and Social Security benefits receding, what's left? Your own personal savings and investment program. We simply cannot continue to rely on the government to sustain tens of millions of people for 10, 20, 30 or 40 years after they retire.

The Value of Planning Ahead

Most people don't plan to fail... they just fail to plan. Sad to say, but most people spend more time planning the details of their next vacation than they do planning the rest of their lives.

"You must have a game plan. If you aim at nothing, you will hit it every time." ~ Anonymous

In sports, coaches devise game plans *before* the game. The game plan usually involves strategies and plays that will allow the players to walk onto the court or field of play with some idea in mind as to how they will proceed. The game plan will be different depending on such things as who the opponent is, what prevailing weather conditions are and how they will likely affect the game. The best coaches are flexible. Opponents plan too, you know. The opposing team may show up with an unexpected offensive or defensive strategy. A smart coach will improvise. The best quarterbacks in football, for example, are experts at calling "audibles."

That's when the signal-caller makes a last-second adjustment in the play to accommodate a change in conditions.

Since the economy is unpredictable, whatever financial plan you have in place needs to be reviewed at least annually to determine if you need to change the game plan. A competent financial advisor will be able to "call an audible" if the signs are present for a shift in the economy that could cause clients to lose a significant portion of their savings. Times change. People change. Circumstances change… sometimes overnight.

With most married couples, either the man or the woman takes care of all the money. The problem with that scenario is, what if the responsible one dies first? It is not uncommon for me to have a conversation with an individual who has recently lost a spouse. In some cases, the deceased spouse is the one who made all the financial decisions for the couple. The surviving spouse doesn't even know how to balance a checkbook. What's wrong with that picture? Proper financial planning should include education so that both partners are financially cared for in case one of them dies. This includes education so that the surviving spouse knows exactly what to do and how to do it. Without such precautions, the consequences can be devastating and traumatic.

The Three Financial Plans Every Couple Needs

Plan A - What if you both live to be 100 years old?

Plan B - What happens to Mrs. if Mr. dies first?

Plan C - What happens to Mr. if Mrs. dies first?

Have you ever seen those glass-encased maps at rest areas along interstate highways? They usually have a big red arrow pointing to a spot on the map, beside which are the words, "YOU ARE HERE." There's a reason for that. You have to know where you are before you can see where you are heading. It's the same with planning your financial future. It starts with a little education about your current situation.

When I first entered the financial services profession, I began to learn that I had a passion for educating people. Sharing what I learn has brought me more joy than anything else associated with my business. When prospective clients decide that they want me to work for them, there comes a point in the process where we need to find that red arrow. We need to discern *where they are* financially. When I ask to see their current investments and they produce their portfolio, I usually ask them some questions. They aren't hard questions. They are questions to which every investor should know the answers:

1) Why do you have this particular investment?

2) How does it work?

3) Do you know what's in your investment?

4) If it's mutual funds, what kind of stocks are in it?

5) If it's bonds, what kind of revenue do you expect?

6) What are the fees? (All the fees! Not just the ones on the surface.)

7) What income can you expect from this investment either now or in the future?

8) What are the tax advantages or disadvantages of this investment?

9) What's your exit strategy?

You need to know the answers to every one of those questions. All too often the three-word answer I hear to so many questions is "I don't know." To put it as plainly as I can, if you don't know, you're either winging it on your own or you're working with the wrong financial professional because they are either unable or unwilling to educate you. I would encourage you to take this list to your current advisor, if you have one, and ask these questions.

If you don't know the answers to these questions, how can you judge if your financial advisor is doing a good job or a poor job? If they're doing a poor job advising you on your finances and you reach retirement only then to find out that you don't have enough to live on, is your *advisor* going to send you a check every month? I don't think so. Therefore, you need an advisor who will educate you and break it down in easy, bite-sized chunks that you can understand and mentally digest.

In this meeting, when we get to the part about the fees, I find that people are surprised to learn just how much they are paying in fees. Sometimes, the fees are buried in the body of all the fine print, or couched in language that makes them invisible. At other times, they are camouflaged — encased in movement of money within the account — so they are not obvious. I enjoy unveiling all the hidden fees of an investment account and enlightening the clients on how much they are paying.

Morningstar Inc. is an investment research firm based out of Chicago, Illinois, that offers an independent analysis of stock market data. I am amazed when we do Morningstar evaluations on certain stocks and mutual funds that are contained in the portfolios of some new clients to see how many of them barely break even. Some of these folks have been riding the stock market roller coaster for decades, and many of them are still in the hole, *hoping* to one day break even. Hope is not a plan.

Probably one of the most important questions: What is your *annualized* rate of return over the last five, 10 or 15 years? Yes, at first glance, this sounds like complicated financial mumbo jumbo but it's actually not. It is extremely important. Your annualized rate of return is essentially how much you've made in an investment over many years and then averaged.

Even if you have an amazing year where you make 12 percent, you may then have a bad year and make 2 percent, followed by a terrible year where you lose 30 percent. In the world of investing in the market, where your returns are rarely consistent, knowing what you've made over a long period of time is the most accurate indicator of successful investing. Can you see now why that question is vital? Knowing the answer to that question can help you determine whether you should stay in that investment or with that advisor.

What many fail to realize is that somebody gets paid whether you make money or not on these types of investments. It has been my observation that many people just "hang in there" because "good ol' George" has been their "guy" for 18 or 26 years. Frankly, if "good ol' George" is not going to be able to personally send you a check for an extra $1,000 per month because your portfolio didn't make enough for you to retire on, then perhaps you should think about seeking advice elsewhere.

My four basic goals of a successful retirement plan today are to:
- Reduce risk
- Reduce fees
- Reduce taxes
- Provide a reasonable rate of return

These are what I call my pillars of success. If what you thought to be true about your investments turned out not to be true, when would you want to know? How about yesterday? I thought so.

However, it's one thing to know something and quite another to do something about it. Human nature resists change. The older we get, the stronger the urge to resist change becomes. For me, the easy part of my job is educating folks. The tough part is getting people to take action on it. A remark that usually gets a chuckle when I am called upon to speak publicly is this: "What is Einstein's definition of insanity? To continue to do exactly what you've always done and expect a different result."

CHAPTER 3

Getting Off the Financial Market Roller Coaster

"Investing should be more like watching paint dry or watching grass grow. If you want excitement, take $800 and go to Las Vegas."
~ Paul Samuelson (1915-2009)

New York had its Coney Island. Los Angeles had its Pacific Ocean Park. We kids in Portland, Oregon, where I grew up in the 1960s, had Jantzen Beach. If the name Jantzen puts you in mind of a swimsuit, there is a connection. Carl Jantzen had been a partner in Portland Knitting Mills when the company was formed in 1910. Jantzen's success with designing swimsuits used by the Portland Rowing Club resulted in the name change to Jantzen Knitting Mills in 1918. When Jantzen and his textile mill partners opened Jantzen Beach Amusement Park in 1928, the crown jewel of the park's rides was to be the biggest roller coaster on the West Coast, named the Big Dipper.

By the time our generation came along, there may have been bigger ones, but we couldn't imagine anything more thrilling than the Dipper. Once you were inside the park, you could ride as many times as you wanted. We couldn't get enough. As soon as one three-minute ride was over, we would line up for another. I can still remember the clickity-clack of the chain as it pulled the car up a vertical incline almost 100 feet high and then dropped us in a virtual freefall to begin our undulating, death-defying ride.

These days, however, I have no desire to be tossed and flung about by a roller coaster or any other contraption. If I go to an amusement park, it will be to perform my grandfatherly duty for Parker, Tyler, Avery, Luke, Blake, Addison or Harper. Even then, I am perfectly content to stroll around and watch them enjoy their moment of terror.

That's the way it is with investing. When we are in our youth, both our portfolios and our psychological makeup can take the thrilling ups and downs of a stock market that is erratic and unpredictable. So what if the market goes down? We didn't have that much to lose anyway. Besides that, it will go back up... eventually. And that's true! It does come back up... eventually. But when we get to the time in our lives when we are approaching retirement, the volatility of the stock market is chilling and uncomfortable. We should have more to lose in market downturns than we did in our early years. The "eventually" part is also a problem for us. We don't have the time to wait for a market to recover from a crash. I have known retired folks who kept their retirement accounts tied solely to the stock market. When the market dips they become edgy. When the market nosedives, they become frantic and worried. If they are using these accounts to fund their retirement, they will stop paying themselves, knowing that each withdrawal is that much less they will have in the account to take advantage of in the next upswing. This restricts their lifestyle. Many of these individuals keep their assets at risk this way because they are unaware there are other investing alternatives that may be safer and can still deliver adequate returns that are capable of generating reliable, sustainable income that you can't outlive.

Dollar Cost Averaging

Young investors can be protected by a force field called "dollar cost averaging" — if, that is, they are consistent and patient. Because time is on their side, they are protected from the volatility of the stock market if they are making regular contributions to their investment accounts. For example, if a younger worker steadily contributes the maximum from his paycheck each week or month into a 401(k) or similar retirement program, those contributions are used by the custodian to buy as many shares in ABC mutual fund as the contribution will buy. I realize that is not the typical diversification 401(k) plans, but I say that just to illustrate the point. What happens if ABC mutual fund shares increase? Wonderful! The account just gained in value. What happens if ABC mutual fund shares go down? Wonderful! Why? Because the contribution will buy more shares. Not to worry. Those shares will come back around *over time,* and remember, time is on the side of the young investor. That's not the case with older folks, however. In fact, the same force field that protected them when they were younger now turns against them and becomes their enemy. They could, if they left all of their money at risk in those mutual funds, be the victim of *reverse* dollar cost averaging. How is that?

Think about it. You stopped collecting paychecks. You no longer contribute to the retirement account. In fact, you are now withdrawing money from the account each month to meet ordinary living expenses. You are in essence writing yourself a paycheck from those funds. Do your expenses stop or decrease if the market fluctuates? No. You go right on withdrawing the same amount each month. Now, with the money stream flowing in the opposite direction as before, instead of *buying* shares, you are *selling* shares. When the share price goes down, you have to sell more shares to net the same pay. When the market picks back up, there is a steadily lessening amount invested to take advantage of the market uptick. It's easy to see why knowing where you are in the stream of time is a key factor in how much risk we take as retired, or nearly retired, investors.

When I first entered the financial profession in March 2000, I drank the "average market return" Kool-Aid that was dispensed during my initial training. Yes, it was true the stock market had historically *averaged* between 8 and 10 percent. But to show a 50-year snapshot of market returns as if it accurately reflects what the market will likely do in the future, especially for retirees, is alarmingly problematic, to say the least.

S&P 500 "Averages"

Year	S&P 500	Average Annual Returns	5-year Avg. Annual Returns	10-year Avg. Annual Returns	15-year Avg. Annual Returns	20-year Avg. Annual Returns	25-year Avg. Annual Returns
1992	7.62%	10.34%	15.88%	16.17%	15.47%	11.33%	10.56%
1993	10.08%	10.33%	14.55%	14.93%	15.72%	12.76%	10.52%
1994	1.32%	10.20%	8.70%	14.38%	14.52%	14.58%	10.98%
1995	37.58%	10.55%	16.59%	14.88%	14.81%	14.60%	12.22%
1996	22.96%	10.71%	15.22%	15.29%	16.80%	14.56%	12.55%
1997	33.36%	11.00%	20.27%	18.05%	17.52%	16.65%	13.07%
1998	28.58%	11.22%	24.06%	19.21%	17.90%	17.75%	14.94%
1999	21.04%	11.35%	28.56%	18.21%	18.92%	17.88%	17.25%
2000	-9.11%	11.05%	18.33%	17.46%	16.02%	15.68%	15.33%
2001	-11.89%	10.71%	10.70%	12.93%	13.74%	15.24%	13.77%
2002	-22.10%	10.21%	-0.59%	9.34%	11.48%	12.71%	12.98%
2003	28.68%	10.43%	-0.57%	11.06%	12.21%	12.98%	13.84%
2004	10.88%	10.43%	-2.30%	12.07%	10.93%	13.22%	13.54%
2005	4.91%	10.36%	0.54%	9.07%	11.52%	11.94%	12.48%
2006	15.79%	10.43%	6.19%	8.42%	10.64%	11.80%	13.37%
2007	5.49%	10.36%	12.83%	5.91%	10.49%	11.82%	12.73%
2008	-37.00%	9.62%	-2.19%	-1.38%	6.46%	8.43%	9.77%
2009	26.46%	9.81%	0.42%	-0.95%	8.04%	8.21%	10.54%
2010	15.06%	9.87%	2.29%	1.41%	6.76%	9.14%	9.94%
2011	2.11%	9.77%	-0.25%	2.92%	5.45%	7.81%	9.28%

http://financeandinvestments.blogspot.com

Showing charts with data from way back in the 20th century, which includes the glory days of the 1980s and 1990s, is false and misleading. Those days are gone. Factoring in those returns falsely raises expectations when it comes to retirement. There is the matter of "sequence of returns" to consider.

Brother A and Brother B

I like to use this example to illustrate this. Let's say we have two brothers, one older and one younger. We will call the older one Brother A and the younger one Brother B. Brother A was fortunate enough to retire in 1991, whereas Brother B retired in 2001. By the time they retired, each brother had accumulated $500,000 in his 401(k) account. Each brother then converted his 401(k) to an IRA account with returns tied directly to the S&P index. When the brothers retired, they each began withdrawing $30,000 per year from their accounts for the next 10 years. Meanwhile, the principal in each account would track the returns of the S&P.

It may help to imagine each of these accounts as a large tank. From a drain at the bottom flows $30,000 each year in withdrawals. From a pipe at the top, positive returns from investments flows. In a year when the investments lose, those losses flow out of the drain at the bottom of the tank.

Can you see why Bother A is the beneficiary of good timing? In the chart that follows, notice how much the market grew during the 1990s. He started out with $500,000 and, 10 years later, ended up with $1,165,530, mainly because of the record gains of the market on the front end of his retirement and because the three years of losses occurred toward the end.

As soon as Brother B retires in 2001, his account is hit with big losses — losses that are draining an account that is already being drained by the $30,000 annual withdrawals. He starts with

$500,000 and 10 years later he has only $306,908 left in his account. That's only about 10 more years' worth of income!

Brother A and Brother B

Year	S&P	Brother A nest egg	Brother B nest egg
1991	-	$500,000	-
1992	7.62%	$508,100	-
1993	10.08%	$529,316	-
1994	1.32%	$506,303	-
1995	37.58%	$666,572	-
1996	22.96%	$789,617	-
1997	33.36%	$1,023,033	-
1998	28.58%	$1,285,416	-
1999	21.04%	$1,525,868	-
2000	-9.11%	$1,356,861	-
2001	-11.89%	$1,165,530	$500,000
2002	-22.10%	$877,948	$359,500
2003	28.68%	$1,099,744	$432,604
2004	10.88%	$1,189,396	$449,671
2005	4.91%	$1,217,795	$441,750
2006	15.79%	$1,380,085	$481,503
2007	5.49%	$1,425,852	$477,937
2008	-37.00%	$868,286	$271,100
2009	26.46%	$1,068,035	$312,834
2010	15.06%	$1,198,881	$329,946
2011	2.11%	$1,194,177	$306,908

Imagine if Brother B had retired in 1999 and had been hit with three consecutive years of significant losses? Even with just one year, Brother B is in danger of running out of money while Brother A is not. Why? Because of something called *sequence of returns*, which simply means the order in which returns are realized.

So when you hear brokers touting the average returns of the market, remember that there is much more involved than that. *Average* is not *actual* when it comes to figuring the growth — or lack of it — in your personal portfolio. Who can predict the sequence of returns on Wall Street? No one. If you have your money in the stock market, you could be the first brother or you could be the second brother. If you are the second brother, maybe your older brother will be kind enough to offer you a loan.

Warren Buffett has two rules. Rule No. 1 is "Never lose money." Rule No. 2 is "Never forget Rule No. 1." That may elicit a chuckle from some, but Buffett, who is widely considered to be the most successful investor in the world, has made billions of dollars in the stock market by conservative investing.

Market Loss Recovery Time

I get puzzled looks sometimes when I say, "The best way to make money is not to lose it in the first place." But it's true. If we could eliminate dramatic losses to our investments, we would be so much better off by far. When people lose a significant portion of their portfolio because they are heavily at risk in stocks, bonds and mutual funds, the consolation offered by brokers is, "Hang in there; the market always comes back." And that may have been true over time. Many labor under the mistaken notion that if they lose 50 percent, then when they make that 50 percent back, they are back to square one. Not true.

Here's a simple way to illustrate this. Take four quarters and place them on a desk or a table. This is your portfolio just before a market crash. For easy math, let's say you lose 50 percent. Remove two of the quarters. Now the market rebounds 50 percent. How many quarters do you put back? One or two? The answer is one. For you to be able to put two quarters back on the table, the market would have had to go up 100 percent, wouldn't it? Losses can be deceiving that way.

As I stated before, the best way to make money is to avoid losing it in the first place. If you are thinking to yourself that a 100 percent gain in the market is rare, you are right. A loss of 50 percent is virtually unsustainable and irrecoverable.

History of Bear Markets

Much of the research from Standard & Poor's, a division of McGraw Hill Financial, is golden when it comes to understanding the behavior of the stock market in the long term.

Since 1929, there have been 16 bear market periods (defined by a 20 percent decline or greater in the S&P 500 Index).

On average, we have a bear market every 4.8 years.

The average depth of a bear market is a 38.24 percent decline in the S&P 500 Index.

The average duration of a bear market is 17 months.

The average time it takes to recover from a bear market is 60 months. That's five years. When we get older and approach retirement, do we really have five years just to break even?

Some periods of economic recession have been of brief duration but very deep. Take 1987, for example. That bear market lasted only three months, but it was very deep as the S&P lost over one-third of its value.

Remember the bear market from March 2000 to October 2002? It was not brief. The S&P plunged 49.1 percent. The recession lasted 31 months, and it took investors 87 months to regain their losses. On Sept. 29, 2008, the Dow Jones Industrial Average lost a record 777 points in one day. Officially, that bear market started in October 2007, and lasted throughout March 2009 — approximately 18 months — but it was the steepest nosedive since the Great

Depression. Some would argue that it was a depression and not a recession. The S&P lost 56.7 percent.[2]

To quote former President Harry S. Truman, "It's a recession if your neighbor loses his job; it's a depression if you lose yours."

In 2013, the Dow broke the 16,000 barrier for the first time! You can almost hear the strains of "We're in the Money," and "Happy Days Are Here Again" on Wall Street. "How long will it last?" you ask. The answer is I don't know. No one knows.

I love the work of political and financial cartoonist Tim Foley, whose insightful and perceptive humor has appeared in The Wall Street Journal, The Boston Globe, New York Newsday and several other prestigious newspapers across the country. When the Dow hit 15,000, Foley drew a celebration scene with confetti, streamers and balloons. Among the celebrants were three bulls dressed in suits, toasting at a punch bowl. As the bulls raise their glasses, we see over on the side of the frame, in a corner, an unsmiling, bearded Ben Bernanke, chairman of the Federal Reserve. Bernanke's caricature is holding a broom and appears to be sweeping up some of the streamers. The Fed chairman is seen glancing over his shoulder where two bulls, dressed in overcoats, are slipping out of the party through a side door. The obvious inference is that the good times the bulls on Wall Street are celebrating may be short lived. The wise cartoonist is subtly making the point that the party on Wall Street may be precariously based on decisions the Federal Reserve makes. It is no secret that the Fed has, at the time of this writing, been buying billions of dollars in U.S. Treasury bonds, which serves to boost liquidity in the economy and keep interest rates artificially low. You get the impression that the bull market will last as long as the Fed allows it to continue. But eventually,

---

[2] Research Financial Strategies. "Understanding the Bulls Versus the Bears." http://www.rfsadvisors.com/Market_Corrections.html.

they will have to take the throttle down on the printing presses and the real economy will emerge.

CHAPTER 4

What's That Hiding in That Mutual Fund?

"The main purpose of the stock market is to make fools of as many men as possible." ~ Bernard Baruch (1890-1965)

Everyone likes a good sleight-of-hand trick. We love to see magicians make things disappear. But when the sleight-of-hand-trick is played on us by someone we trust and what disappears is our money, we are not so amused! Are there hidden fees lurking in the fine print of our financial statements? I don't know who the people are personally who lay out and prepare these financial statements, but judging from some of them that cross my desk for review, I am convinced they must have taken special courses on obfuscation and concealment. "Who reads the fine print, right?"

I know some people who don't even open the envelopes containing their account statements. They just stack them up in chronological order and procrastinate until they finally have to file them away. One couple, after attending one of my educational workshops on retirement income planning conducted shortly after the 2008 market crash, came into the office the next afternoon for a consultation. They brought with them a box with several unopened envelopes containing statements from their stockbroker. When I asked them why they hadn't opened the envelopes, the man spoke up and said, "We know there is bad news in there." And there was! Their broker had placed them in risky market positions, either disregarding their advanced age or not noticing it, which had cost them more than a third of their life's savings.

Bank statements are usually pretty straightforward, but you should at least scan them for charges you may not have agreed to. One woman who started using an online bill pay program provided by her bank didn't realize that it came with a $15 fee attached. Pay attention to minimum balance accounts. One slip below the line and fees can add up quickly. Please don't be embarrassed to ask questions of any financial organization that charges fees. "Why was I charged this, and what can I do to avoid this fee in the future?" Dollars add up to hundreds of dollars and hundreds add up to thousands. Don't forget, these people work for you, and they make profits based on the money you have in your account.

How about the credit cards in your wallet? Why do you have *those* particular credit cards? If you carry a balance (not always recommended) on your credit cards, how much interest do the credit card companies charge? Do you pay them off each month? Good! One client told me that he always pays off his credit cards as soon as he gets the bills, but he got a nasty surprise from one of his credit card companies when he returned from vacation one month. Because he had neglected to pay his bill on time, the card company slapped a late fee of $45 on the account and bumped up the APR from 8 percent to 18 percent.

"They waived the late fee when I called to complain," he said, adding that he paid the balance and canceled the card forthwith. Credit card companies are notorious for levying charges and fees once you owe a balance. If you carry a balance on your credit card, why not shop for the card that has the lowest APR (annual percentage rate)? These cards typically do not offer the fancy rewards programs but they usually do not charge an annual fee. If you are one who pays off your balance every month, and you like the air miles or cash back, etc., that's fine. As with all things financial, there is no free lunch. The credit card companies are in business to make a profit.

I will share this last thing about credit card companies with you. They negotiate. If you are happy with the service you receive from the card company but think you're paying too much in interest and fees, why not call the credit card issuer to see if they will match or beat the terms and rate on the new card you're considering?

Take It Line by Line

Back to the couple with the unopened envelopes. In order to help them understand their statements, we took the most recent one and put it on the projector in the conference room and went down the entries line by line. That's how to do it. Take your time. Read each word of each page of one statement. If you don't understand some phrase or expression, ask questions of your financial advisor until you do understand it. Call the company that generated the statement. If you get an, "I don't know," you're talking to the wrong person. Ask for a supervisor until you get an explanation that is crystal clear to you. Don't feel intimidated or embarrassed to admit you don't know what something means. It's your money, not theirs. They are handsomely paid by you for their service. Remember, they work for you!

The husband and wife in my conference room were intrigued by the world of information contained in their statements. They were also a little angry. Not only had they lost money in their account, they had paid the brokerage house handsomely for the privilege! No wonder the statements aren't easy to comprehend.

Beware of Hidden Mutual Fund Fees

Mutual funds are popular in America. According to the Investment Company Institute, more than half of all households owned a mutual fund, and assets in mutual funds totaled $11.6 trillion in 2011. We understand the idea behind them. They are designed to allow the average investor to diversify and invest en masse so as to have the advantages of larger investors. With millions of American workers pumping money into 401(k) plans every month, and with that river of cash dumping right into the mutual fund ocean, it's no wonder they are so big. But do people really know what they are buying? Mutual funds had some advantages at one time, but anymore, with the onset of rapid trading via computers and ETFs (exchange traded funds), are they really all they were cracked up to be? Many in my profession think not.[3]

Here is a quote from Forbes magazine: "Most mutual funds are plagued by more drawbacks than benefits — they've become inefficient and largely outdated investment vehicles." The magazine goes on to list the following four areas in which mutual funds are inefficient: (a) Poor performance relative to indexing, (b) tax inefficient (c) difficult to manage, and (d) excessive costs.[4]

Defined contribution plans such as 401(k)s hold the largest share of mutual funds in America. How did that come about? Teresa Ghilarducci, director of the Schwartz Center for Economic

---

[3] Investment Company Institute. "2013 Investment Company Fact Book." 53rd Edition.

[4] Bill Harris. Forbes. June 7, 2012. "Four Ways Mutual Funds Hurt Your Retirement." http://www.forbes.com/sites/billharris/2012/06/07/four-ways-mutual-funds-hurt-your-retirement.

Policy Analysis at The New School for Social Research, is quite candid about 401(k)s and the myriad of mutual funds they contain. In an article that appeared in the online magazine FRONTLINE on April 13, 2013, she called the 401(k) system a "failed experiment" for middle-class Americans because it was never designed with them in mind.

"It's not the fault of people that they don't have enough savings in their individual retirement account or their 401(k)s," she said. "It's the fault of the system, and the whole system needs to be reformed." She called 401(k)s, and by association the mutual funds they contain, "the only products that Americans buy without knowing [their] true cost."

To understand where we are with mutual funds in America, we have to go back to the passage of ERISA, the Employee Retirement Income Security Act of 1974. It was a time when people started losing their pensions after many years of working for a company who had now gone bankrupt and had no money with which to keep their pension promises. The most notorious example was that of the Studebaker automobile manufacturing company. (You may be a baby boomer if you ever rode in a Studebaker). The company was really ahead of its time, but America wasn't ready for some of its innovations. The sleek Studebaker was the first to have seatbelts in every car, and it came out with the first power steering. But the car was a flop with the fickle American car-buying public and Studebaker went bankrupt and couldn't pay its pensions. The last Studebaker rolled off the line in 1966. Some folks had worked for 30 and 40 years making Studebakers and were left holding the bag. Studebaker's ex-employees and other workers with the same problem complained loudly to Congress, which led to the passage of ERISA in 1974. This new law, intended to force corporations to back up their pensions, led to another law passed in 1978 that would dramatically change how Americans prepared for retirement — The Revenue Act of 1978.

Enter the 401(k)

Few noticed this new legislation contained a section 401, paragraph (k) that permitted American workers to save money for retirement and lower their taxes at the same time. But the wording did not escape the notice of Ted Benna, a Philadelphia benefits consultant who saw that it allowed for bonuses that could be tax-deferred if saved for retirement. Benna noticed nothing in the law that said that regular wages could receive the same tax treatment, and the 401(k) was born. He had to get this approved by the IRS, which finally came through in the spring of 1981. The 401(k) quickly began spreading across the country, eventually replacing pensions. Similar salary-deferral retirement plans are authorized in the tax code for public-sector employees (known as 457 plans) and nonprofit-sector employees (known as 403(b) plans).

There are advantages and disadvantages to the 401(k). The money you put into it is tax-deferred as it grows. Money you would have been paying in taxes grows at compound interest. What a sweet deal, right? Compounding means you would be earning interest on the interest of the interest on the interest.

But, like chickens coming home to roost, the taxes will eventually be paid when you began using the money for its intended purpose — retirement. Put that down as a disadvantage. Tax-deferred doesn't mean tax-free. Uncle Sam was making us all a deal that, when you think about it, he couldn't lose. Let's say that you are a farmer walking into a store to buy seed for the spring crop. Over by the checkout counter is Uncle Sam in his stars-and-stripes suit, wearing a hat that says IRS.

"I will make you a deal, young fellow," Uncle Sam says, extending his hand. "I won't charge you a penny on this seed, but you pay me full bore on the harvest."

Most of us took the deal. Assuming your account grows, the IRS will be rewarded handsomely for waiting. Not only that, but when you leave what you don't use to your heirs, they may have to pay both income tax and estate tax on the amount received, subject to current tax laws.

Another thing, pensions were guaranteed for life. The balance in a 401(k) account is usually invested in mutual funds by a custodian, such as Vanguard or Fidelity. Are they subject to the volatility of the stock market? Yes, indeed. Just ask some who lost as much as 50 percent of their account value during the last stock market crash.

Since 401(k)s are so heavily invested in mutual funds, many American workers don't realize how much they are paying in fees.

We would all like to go to sleep at night with the knowledge that our money is safe and that the people who are handling it for us will be open and forthright with us. I think we call that "transparency." But that is just not always the case. And the people who work in the Obfuscation Department bury these fees for a reason. When the market is down and you are losing, they would like for you not to notice them. It's better for them if fees and charges fade into the background and disappear into the sea of other information on the page, sort of like camouflage in a forest.

It would be nice, of course, if you could open your statements and see a large headline that read, "**FEES and OTHER CHARGES**," at the top of a page and then have all the fees and charges printed there in 22-point type. It would go a long way toward restoring our faith in the money changers at the Wall Street temple, but don't hold your breath.

Broker Fees

Brokers charge fees that can be called anything from "confirmation fees" to "annual maintenance fees," and they are not always easy to spot. You often have to get out your high-powered reading glasses or go to the website to find them. Here are just a few examples:

IRA Custodial Fees – This is where a discount broker charges you either to keep your account with them or to close the account. They sometimes waive the fee for large accounts. It hardly seems fair, since they are making money with your money and every movement of your money within the account.

Fees to Close Your IRA – This is a way to persuade you not to switch accounts. Transfer your IRA to another custodian and you will usually pay between $30 and $125.

Confirmations and Paper Statements – It apparently saves brokerage houses money when you go paperless. I get that. And they will sometimes sell you on that using an ecological pitch about wasting natural resources, trees being one. But if you're like me, I like to receive a paper statement. It surely won't kill too many redwoods in the rain forest for me just to have the comfort and peace of mind of receiving a piece of paper that I can read and file away when I'm through. What if the Internet service is down? (It happens.) What if your email provider mistakes the statement for spam and kicks it into the junk mail folder and you delete it by mistake? We are starting to see companies charging $5 just for sending you a paper statement!

Annual Maintenance Fees – If you have less than $30,000 in your account, and you aren't a frequent trader, you may get hit with an annual maintenance fee ranging anywhere from $100 per year to $25 per month.

Fees to Transfer Your Account – It is odd how this one works out. They may not be returning your phone calls and they may be charging fees and commissions that are too high, but they still don't want to lose your business. This fee, which is usually around $50 to $125, is tacked on to discourage you from going somewhere else.

"A mutual fund is really there for people who have already saved enough for their retirement and in an institutional long-term investment product, who have already paid off their house and want to take their money and top off their [security] base for retirement," said Ghilarducci.

"It's not an appropriate product for people who need to save a part of their paycheck every time they receive one in order to have money for a long-term need for the rest of their lives."

A Shares, B Shares and C Shares

When checking for different quotes on mutual funds, you might see different prices for classes of mutual fund shares that seem to be holding similar or identical products. These different classes — 'A', 'B' and 'C' — all are characterized by their different load structures.

Shares designated as 'A' shares generally denote a front-load charge. This load is generally fixed for the duration of the fund and will vary depending on the different types of mutual funds. Fund companies recognize that the front load is a deterrent to investors, so to sweeten the attractiveness of the fund, they may reduce the management expense ratios (MER). Thus, some funds claim that, even though you are paying a large fee up front, you will end up saving money if you decide to hold this fund for a long duration.

The 'B' shares normally are deferred-load funds. In many instances, this deferred load will dissipate along a schedule so the longer you hold the fund, the smaller the deferred load becomes. When the deferred fund no longer has back-end charges, it will normally be reclassified as an 'A' share. It may seem advantageous to purchase and hold the 'B' class until the load structure completely dissolves, but this is not necessarily the case. Fund companies may circumvent lost profits by charging a higher MER.

The 'C' shares are constant-load funds. Regardless of the number of years the fund is held, the load charge is present. Since this fund's load is lower than both the 'A' and 'B' classes, it generally also has a higher expense ratio to offset the fund company's lost revenue; furthermore, 'C' shares typically do not reclassify into 'A' shares, which means the purchaser of these shares will be stuck paying the full load when he or she sells the fund.

Keep in mind that fund companies will designate their multi-class mutual funds differently, but the letters we refer to above are the most common classifications. When you are looking to purchase a new fund, it's definitely important that you understand the load structure and availability of different classes. Also, remember that loads do not automatically get you a higher return. In fact, most evidence suggests that no-load funds are usually a better choice.

For people who come into our office at Northwest Financial & Tax Solutions, Inc., we do Morningstar reports and let them see for themselves all the fees that they are paying on their current investments. Sometimes the truth hurts. But it is also the light of the world. If you were paying as much as $150,000 over a lifetime in fees and charges, when would you want to know about it? If you said "immediately," you are spot on! It's so important that you know these things because it can absolutely affect the trajectory and timing of your retirement. One of the goals of any financial planner who is a true fiduciary is to educate clients on how they can *reduce* fees, not pay more of them. Whenever you partner with any investment advisor, they are getting paid, one way or another. Do you know how yours is getting paid? Some advisors charge you for meeting with them, some are fee only, some work on a commission basis, some are remunerated with commissions and fees, some are paid by the hour and some are paid salary plus bonus.

CHAPTER 5

In Pursuit of Retirement Success

I'm neither a psychologist nor a sociologist. I'm a financial guy, and my job is to work with my clients to create a comprehensive financial plan that helps them accomplish their goals. But life is multifaceted. Success in retirement may mean different things to different people.

Socially, for example, our best friends may be the people down at the office — the office we are leaving behind. Retiring will be a big transition for those whose social world revolves around workmates and professional associates. For some, the job defines them. Not working can give them an identity crisis.

Psychologically, there are some people who need to work. Retirement is a time to follow your passions. But if your passion is your work, then you have to carve out a new niche. Many retirees these days start their own businesses — not because they need the money, but because they feel they have a lot more to contribute to society. I know one man who loved to tinker in his garage. His day job was being a bank president, but he loved building things, particularly working with wood. After he retired, he got a very low-paying job at a local hardware store. He was the man with the helpful hardware plan, or whatever that Ace Hardware jingle used to say. You could bring virtually any household maintenance challenge to him and he could tell you how to conquer it and show you in which aisle you could find the hardware for the job. People loved him and he loved the job. There are different strokes for different folks when it comes to retirement success. There may be significant tax advantages to setting up your own business, like being able to write off business and travel expenses.

Physically, people often change their lifestyle habits after retirement. Some for the better. They exercise more. Some take up tennis, biking or hiking. Others for the worse. One study revealed that people who retired involuntarily tended to drink more alcohol than they did before retirement. Another effect retirement has in some is added stress. It may sound counterintuitive, but the stress comes from losing daily control and stepping out of a tightly scheduled routine into one where time moves more slowly from day to day.

Retirement is a big adjustment **emotionally and psychologically**. Couples who have been together for decades but have the daily diversions of careers may have to get used to being together more often. Privacy may have to be redefined. As I said, I don't specialize in this field, but those who do tell me that couples should talk through this change in their lives and use it as an opportunity to grow together, instead of grow apart. Each spouse may learn the other's hobbies and interests and even join in them.

Financially, there are several additional factors that play into a person's retirement success. Like I said, I have no degrees in psychology or mental health, and my knowledge about the other facets of retirement are limited to my own personal experience (which is considerable) and what I have read and learned from listening to the stories of thousands of clients. But according to the plaques hanging on my office wall and the letters sprinkled after my name on my business card, I do have a working knowledge about the financial side of retirement, and I can confirm this to be true: Being financially *comfortable* in retirement beats being financially uncomfortable hands down.

Have you ever noticed the smiling faces of the people on the cover of retirement brochures? Because I keep my ear close to the ground on all matters pertaining to financial planning for people who are either retired or approaching retirement, I get dozens of periodicals and brochures from various media sources and companies every month. All the illustrations in this literature are similar in theme: A casually dressed 60-something couple strolls down the beach, the sun behind them, low in the sky, golden sunlight glinting off the ocean (there seems to always be a beach or a sailboat in these pictures). The two are sweetly holding hands. Grandchildren are playing nearby. Oh, yes, there is usually a dog in the photograph, usually a big, friendly dog, like a Labrador retriever. And everyone is smiling, even the dog. Sometimes the woman will have her head back, caught in a moment of laughter while the wind tosses her salt-and-pepper hair. These people are thin and healthy with perfect teeth, and all of them seem to have that hip senior look. Just the kind of people you think it would be fun to vacation with.

These happy people are only models, of course, hired for a photo shoot. But they must be representative of what the ideal retirement should be. The people in these photographs are not plagued with money worries. No furrowed brows here, wondering if they will be able to pay next month's utilities. They are financially well set and enjoying their golden years in financial freedom. This is not just an elusive fantasy. I enjoy using actual photographs of my clients on my website. They are happy, thriving and active; all they have to do is act naturally!

Don't Worry; Be Happy

Will Rogers was an American cowboy, vaudeville performer, humorist, social commentator and movie star. He was a real celebrity in the 1920s and 1930s and was famous for taking humorous pokes at Wall Street and Congress. Here's a sampling:

"Why don't somebody print the truth about our present economic situation? We spent six years of wild buying on credit — everything under the sun, whether we needed it or not — and now we are having to pay for 'em, and we are howling like a pet coon."

"The whole financial structure of Wall Street seems to have fallen on the mere fact that the Federal Reserve Bank raised the amount of interest from 5 to 6 percent. Any business that can't survive a 1 percent raise must be skating on mighty thin ice ... But let Wall Street have a nightmare and the whole country has to help get them back in bed again."

Sound familiar? It appears not much has changed, doesn't it? Rogers' humor would hit the mark today as accurately as it did back in the days of the Great Depression when he appeared before audiences and his poignant humor made them chuckle at the nation's prevailing misery.

Another quote that is attributed to the rope-twirling Rogers is: *"In retirement, I am more concerned with the return _of_ my principal than the return _on_ my principal."*

I remember some senior citizens getting quite excited a few years ago, when CD rates skyrocketed back up to 5 percent. But at that time, after you paid taxes and factored in inflation, you might have been breaking even at 5 percent... maybe. What do CDs return these days? One thing is certain: If you are receiving four-tenths of 1 percent, you are losing money due to inflation every day your money is in the bank. So why do some seniors still keep their money in such a low-return environment as CDs? Because they are afraid of the risk that goes along with having it in the stock market. So what about risk? What can you do about it?

What Can You Do About Risk?

Essentially, there are four things you can do with risk:

Accept it. Most people just accept risk because they think that's all they can do. They have been trained to think, "no pain, no gain." To them, risk is like the weather. You will have periods of rain followed by drought. It may snow. The winds will blow. And there isn't one thing you can do about it, so you just live with it. It's kind of like gambling. If you win, you win. If you lose, well, that's the breaks of investing. I have to confess, there was a time in my life — prior to really getting educated — that I thought that way, too. But it's simply not the case.

Buy-and-hold no longer works. This is the age of computer trading and rapid response in the market. During the 2008 market crash, the ones who lost the most were the ones who put their faith in the buy-and-hold investing philosophies of yesteryear.

In the 1990s, you could have dressed up a monkey in a clown suit and had him throw darts at a board and bought the stocks where the dart landed and done pretty well. They called it the tech boom. There are several crazy stories from that era, but one of the most fascinating, and unfortunately rather typical, is the one of Mark Cuban and Broadcast.com. Broadcast.com was founded to let people listen to radio broadcasts over the Internet. In 1998, however, so few people had broadband access that few ever actually heard anything on the site. In April 1999, Yahoo acquired the company for $5.7 billion, making Cuban a lot of money. But the company never took off... and now it doesn't exist. Cuban is still around. In fact, he used his millions to buy the Dallas Mavericks, a National Basketball Association franchise.

It was a case of too much, too fast. The IPOs (initial public offerings) of Internet companies emerged with ferocity and frequency, sweeping the nation up in euphoria. Investors were blindly grabbing every new issue. Few thought to look at a business plan to find out, for example, how long it would take the new companies to actually begin making a profit. Companies that couldn't decide on their corporate creed were given millions of dollars and told to grow to Microsoft size by tomorrow. The holes in the bubble began to appear when many of these overnight wonders reported huge losses. Some folded within months of their public offering. The founders of these companies, the "Siliconaires" as they were called, had to pack up and move out of their $4 million mansions and move back in with their parents. In 1999, there were 457 IPOs, most of which were Internet and technology related. Of those 457 IPOs, 117 doubled in price on the first day of trading. In 2001, the number of IPOs dwindled to 76, and none of them doubled on the first day of trading.

Fortunately, I was able to get out of the stock market before it started plunging, thanks to some sage advice I received as a teenager. A wise old man once told me, "When it comes to investing, never give back more than 10 percent." I suppose I also have my conservative upbringing to thank. I can still hear my mother's words, "If it sounds too good to be true, it probably is." Had it not been for the "buy and hold" philosophy still stuck in the minds of investors, many others would have recognized this market was behaving like none before it.

I entered the financial services profession in March 2000, four days before the peak of the market — a time some would later say couldn't have been any worse. The "corrections" of 2000, 2001 and 2003 were eye-opening for me. Another event occurred during that period that let the investing world know just how quickly things could change and how suddenly markets could be negatively affected. America was attacked by terrorists who had hijacked passenger jets and flown them like bombs into the twin towers of the World Trade Center. To prevent a stock market meltdown, the New York Stock Exchange and the Nasdaq closed for a week, from Sept. 11 through Sept. 17, 2001. I set out with a goal to be the top retirement planning specialist in America. After the events of 9/11, I was determined to never be in a position where I was sitting across the table from nice people who trusted me with their money trying to explain what happened to it. The world we live in today is just too volatile.

The residual effect of that shocker was that it changed everything I thought I knew about investing. After 9/11, I knew I could no longer use the philosophies that I had used in the past. Portfolio diversification is a good thing, but I could no longer accept the doctrine preached by the brokerage houses that merely spreading your risk among different asset classes was enough to safeguard your assets from risk in a stock market meltdown. Their mantra was that if your investments were spread out according to a formula — so much in large cap stocks, so much in small cap stocks, so much in international stocks, so much in growth stocks — you couldn't be hurt. The events of 9/11 changed all of that. Why? Picture yourself standing in a canoe. It's a beautiful day. The lake is calm. Your feet are set wide apart. You are balanced perfectly. Occasionally, you cast your line into the lake hoping for a trout or bass. I did say that you are standing in a canoe, right? But it's okay, because you are balanced and stable. Your weight is evenly distributed. All is going well until, you guessed it, some yahoos in a speed boat out for a joy ride roar by and kick up the waves. You frantically shift your weight to keep your stance, but you can't move fast enough. As you fight for equilibrium, the boat moves beneath you. That balanced distribution doesn't help you. The canoe tips, and you are in the water.

As it turns out, this same lesson applies to investment portfolios. Harry Markowitz is best known for his investing theory of the 1950s that contended that diversification could mitigate, or at least minimize, market volatility. That theory suffers from the same problems a man standing balanced in a canoe would have. Correlations between stocks *change* when the markets move up or down rapidly. What happened in 2001-2003 had never happened before. If the market suddenly plunges downward, you would hope that your well-diversified portfolio, invested as it is in stocks that tend to move unlike one another, would be safe. But when markets move *significantly* down, or up, it turns out the correlations are no longer what they were. Trending markets induce strong correlations among stocks that weren't there beforehand. Long-term averages don't work anymore. So the risks to a portfolio are actually much larger than the simple diversification analysis suggests — just as the risk of a canoe tipping is much more than it seems to a man standing balanced on a peaceful lake.

Portfolio diversification and buy-and-hold strategies are old investing habits that represent the past but they are hard to dislodge. When investors put their assets in investments that are *all correlated* to the stock market, whether in the S&P 500, the Dow, the Nasdaq or any other exchange that reflects the value of the stock market, they are essentially accepting the full risk of the stock market. Just because their portfolio contains a mixture (small cap, large cap, international funds, bonds, etc.) does not mean they are diversified. They are still fully at risk.

"But isn't that just part of investing?" some may ask. That is what some who are in the business of selling shares of stock would like you to believe. Here's the way one broker explained things to a couple who were on the verge of retirement when a sudden market drop cost them a small fortune of their invested savings.

BROKER: "I'm sorry you lost so much money in your investments, but relax. You're not alone. You know that when the tide goes out, all the boats in the harbor go down. Then when the tide comes back in, all the boats rise again. So just hold on; the market will recover."

That may sound good, but it just doesn't wash. The 2008 market crash was no tide going out. It was the entire ocean backing miles away from shore and leaving all the boats in the mud!

There was a time when the market would recede and advance, somewhat like the tides — a dependable pattern that was not too risky. But with the passing of the 1990s, the stock market has been much too volatile to trust with a buy-and-hold approach. We live in an age of round-the-clock financial news and information. A disturbance in one hemisphere is instantly registered on another, oceans away. This can lead to tremendous volatility. It no longer makes sense to buy a stock and check on its performance a year later. The days of active portfolio management are here. Money managers must be nimble enough to get in and get out of positions so as to mitigate loss. What we once referred to as "buy and hold," I now call "buy and *hope!*" You buy and hope it's worth something down the road when you need it.

Reduce it. Another way you can handle market risk is to reduce it. How do you reduce risk? One way is to explore alternative investments that are not correlated with the stock market. There are investments of this sort. Take nonpublicly traded real estate investment trusts (REITs), for example. These are viable investments but they are not based in the stock market. REITs, like anything that can increase or decrease in value, comprise risk — just not *market* risk (until they go public). When bonds fade and stocks rise, the market tends to regard REITs as if they were dividend-paying growth stocks. It's only when just about everything is tanking, as was the case in 2008, that publicly traded REITs get hammered. I am not necessarily recommending REITs, I'm just pointing out there are alternative investments that, if you want to reduce risk by diversification, you may consider.

Another investment that is not market related is equipment leasing. Again, I am not recommending equipment leasing, but it is an investment program that is outside the stock market. If you are unfamiliar with the concept, equipment leasing funds invest in a portfolio of equipment essential to business, such as trucks, cranes, bulldozers and other tangible assets. A delivery company, such as FedEx or UPS, for example, may find that it is financially beneficial to lease its trucks instead of buying them. Sometimes "big ticket" items, such as ships, barges, rail cars or aviation equipment, fall into this category. It may not be for every investor, but it can produce a regular income and certain tax advantages. It could be a partial inflation hedge, but remember, they are not guaranteed.

Other alternatives to market investing can be some forms of life insurance and some kinds of annuities in which there is predictable growth and virtually no risk. The closer we get to retirement, the more attractive annuities become. Retirees who have too much money in equities face the risk that the stock market will continue falling at the very same time they are withdrawing money from their accounts. This course dramatically increases the odds they will outlive their money. Of course, an alternative would be for them to reduce their withdrawals and, with them, their standard of living, but it is not an option most want to consider. Those who retired in the investing euphoria of the late 1990s and believed the joyride would never end learned firsthand what can happen if you leave your assets solely in equities.

The U.S. Government Accountability Office (GAO) produced a 79-page report in 2006 that recommended annuities as part of a retirement strategy. The report recommended that to avoid an unfavorable "sequence of returns" in the securities' markets, seniors should consider investing between 5 and 25 percent of their portfolios in stocks and buying a life annuity. The GAO recommended the more obvious measures of saving more, working longer, investing wisely and delaying Social Security payments as long as possible.

One reason I am citing the suggestions of the GAO when it comes to annuities is because they are not biased. They have nothing to gain by recommending them. The GAO is not in any way connected to the insurance industry. Annuities have been bashed by those brokerage houses and others who promote the notion that investing in equities is the only way to build and maintain wealth. They, of course, are biased. More and more, the media is waking up to annuities as a viable part of a retirement investment portfolio. Fox Business published an article in 2012 titled "The Top 3 Annuity Myths and Truths Behind Them," in which the author states he likes annuities because they serve their purpose. "They'll pay you guaranteed, down to the penny, a series of monthly payments no matter how long you live," the article states, referring to them as "modern personal pensions." He also exposes the following myths about annuities:

Myth No. 1: *Annuities are too confusing.*

The Fox Business writer says many are surprised when he tells them an annuity works just like a company pension or Social Security benefits. You agree to set some of your retirement savings aside, and the company with the annuity promises to pay you a lifetime income.

A brief side note about the author's point: If you invest your money in a fixed index annuity with an income rider, you can keep your principal or the money you invest intact and have the opportunity to see some of the benefits of the rise of a market index such as the S&P 500 with no threat to the loss of your principal or the money you originally invested. Also, the money is still yours and can be passed down to your heirs in its entirety.

Myth No. 2: *Insurance companies keep the remaining money when you die.*

With the exception of an immediate annuity (there are many kinds of annuities), this is simply not true. Immediate annuities don't spend any time in deferral or gaining interest and within 30 days provide you with income, but the income payments cease at your demise. But with fixed index annuities, you pass along any and all remaining money in your account probate free to your beneficiaries.

Myth No. 3: *Annuities have high and hidden ongoing fees.*

The only annuities that have fees are variable annuities, which we do not like. They have fees because they are equity vs. insurance. With fixed index annuities, you only have a fee if you want an income rider. That fee is usually less than 1 percent and considered nominal for the benefits provided. You are paying a fee to know you may live long enough to run out of money but you can never run out of income! Traditional investments, like stocks, bonds or mutual funds, cannot guarantee that. What's more, you can take on all the risk of those traditional investments, pay lots more in fees and still have no guarantees.

The Fox Business article had more to say, but that is the essence of it. The fact is you will always know what the fees are up front when it comes to annuities. When it comes to reducing risk, there is no cookie-cutter answer and no silver bullet. Every situation is different. I strongly encourage you to see a retirement income specialist who can acquaint you with all your options. Can you do it yourself? Of course. It's a free country and the Internet makes research so available that you are only limited by your curiosity and your ability to separate food from fodder. But I don't recommend do-it-yourself investing any more than I would consider giving myself an X-ray or performing complex automobile repairs. Remember, you are looking for *alternatives* to market risk, not more of the same. The key question is, "How much of my money is guaranteed?" If your financial advisor doesn't know what you're talking about, then you are probably in the wrong place talking to the wrong person.

Transfer it. Another way to handle investment risk is to transfer it. Insurance is designed to transfer risk. We all have different forms of insurance for the various perils from which we wish to protect ourselves. If the house burns down, you don't want to have to go to your bank and pull out your savings to rebuild. So you have fire insurance. Now you have transferred that risk to an insurance company. The same goes for your cars. You have risk because you drive and the roads are dangerous. What if you have an accident and damage your automobile? Worse yet, what if you injure someone? Again, you transfer that risk to an insurance company when you pay your premiums. The same goes with health insurance.

You can transfer investment risk as well by transferring some of your assets to products that give you guarantees. Have you ever bought an appliance and when you went to pay for it the clerk asked you if you wished to purchase an extended warranty? The warranty cost you something, didn't it? Did you weigh the pros and cons in your mind before you answered yes or no? Most people do. It's just another of life's little choices. If your investment comes with a guarantee, you will give up something in return for that guaranteed return. You will, in some way, shape or form, pay something for that added security. But it may be worth it. This is especially true if you are approaching retirement and your resources turn from renewable to nonrenewable. Generally speaking, guarantees are more attractive than projections to those who are in the "retirement red zone" (five years on either side of your retirement date).

Manage it. If you have ever been to a large art museum, you probably noticed the gigantic size of some paintings. Some of them cover an entire wall. When you stand close to them, it's difficult to see what the painting is all about. You have to back up and get the big picture. To get an accurate picture of the stock market, you have to back up and look at it over time. You can see the patterns better and that can help you manage risk.

As this book is written in October 2015, the Dow is at 17,000, the Nasdaq is at 4,700 and the S&P is at 2,000. Driven by what? A healthy economy!

Such was not always the case, however. In our rearview mirror is what some market watchers call the "lost decade" of 2000-2010

— so called because market advances were negated by the declines. It is during periods like this that you must manage your risk very carefully.

During the period of 1982 to 2000, the people who, as they say, "got the biggest bang for their buck" were those with the "buy-and-hold" approach. They would buy stock, a mutual fund, for example, and hold onto it, confident of good returns. That works well when we are in a clearly defined bull market. But, in a sideways market — where the market declines for two or three years, goes up for three or four years, then goes down for a couple of years, then back up for three or four years — when you stand back and look at the pattern, you are, after all that time, essentially back where you started. A lot of activity and very little accomplishment. Jogging in place.

Paper Gain Versus Paper Loss

The philosophy we are advocating here is simply this: Employ a strategy that reduces, transfers and manages risk all at the same time. We think merely accepting it, as if there were no other choices, is not a viable option. If times have changed in the investing world, why is it that some keep investing the same old way?

In 1888, the football rules were changed to allow tackling below the waist. The safety concern was offset by requiring the players to wear padded uniforms. But helmets were still optional. A few concussions later, in 1939, they were made mandatory in college games. The professional ranks were hard-headed. They waited until 1943 to require them. The old helmets were flimsy affairs, made of leather with cloth padding inside. The plastic football helmet came along in 1940. It was stronger, lighter and offered more protection, and within a year, the leather helmets were a thing of the past. Modern plastic helmets are pretty high-tech affairs with air bladders and custom-fitted padding inside.

Just as it would be unthinkable to march out onto the football playing field without a helmet, it is senseless to use the same old investing methods of yesteryear in today's fast-paced stock market. There's no other way to put it. Advisors who insist on using the two-lane back roads instead of the interstate are giving their clients a bum steer. It's like a coach sending a player into the game with inferior equipment.

CHAPTER 6

Losing Money When You Shouldn't

The best way to make money is to not lose it in the first place. That may sound like just another clever expression, but I am dead serious. We live in an information age with knowledge at our fingertips through the media and the Internet, and yet there are still many investors who have antiquated views. One expression I hear often at client appreciation dinners is: "Before we met you, we thought there were only two places to put money — into the banks or the stock market." That seems to be a common misimpression. One is a wild ride and the other is a dead end, at least as far as investment is concerned, so they are really not happy with either one. Are you? But to their way of thinking, based on the information they have at hand, what choice do they have?

I think that's why so many investors take the losses of the stock market, even some that are devastating, with a kind of glum resignation, as if to say, "That's the breaks of the investing game."

When we do Morningstar evaluations on the portfolios of prospective clients, I am always amazed at how many of them are 100 percent stocks and mutual funds. Many of these individuals have been riding the market roller coaster for years and don't seem to know how to get off. Some of them have barely broken even. Others are still in the hole. You must know what your annualized rate of return (ARR) is over the last five, 10 or 15 years.

One thing I learned in corporate America, years before I entered the financial services industry, is that if you want to know why something happens in any commercial endeavor, just follow the money trail. There is usually a profit motive to everything that moves in the free market monetary stream. To put it plainly, the brokers get paid whether the investments made money or not. The difference between a broker and an advisor is straightforward. Brokers help match buyers and sellers in exchange for a commission. That's true whether you are talking about real estate or rare fish. When it comes to investing in the stock market, the size of a traditional broker's paycheck is based on the volume of transactions brokered. So, if no trades take place, the broker doesn't get paid, regardless of whether he or she provided any investment advice to clients. There is some debate in the financial services community as to who should be able to use the designation "advisor." When I use the term "advisor," I mean someone operating as a fiduciary, who puts their clients' best interests at the heart of their financial advice. Generally speaking, brokers do not have a fiduciary responsibility to clients.

When you invest in fee-based products, however, you receive the benefit of ongoing consultation with a professional financial advisor in exchange for a predictable fee. The advisor is responsible for managing your financial plan, which includes examining your overall financial situation, determining your risk tolerance, helping you set goals, recommending an asset allocation that is appropriate for your goals, assisting with investment selection and monitoring your portfolio and the progress toward your goals. Keep in mind that most traditional advisors will rise and fall together with market cycles. If they do not produce your desired results, you choose whether you wish to continue to employ them.

Because the advisor is paid based on a percentage of assets under management, he or she has a personal stake in the success of your portfolio. For example, if your advisor's fee is 1 percent and your portfolio contains $100,000, he or she earns $1,000 per year. If your portfolio grows to $200,000, that same 1 percent fee is now worth $2,000. Clearly, the advisor has a financial incentive to seek out the best asset allocation instead of only selling products that pay high commissions. This arrangement lessens the investor's concern over churning, and ensures advisors play for the same team as their clients — both client and advisor stand to win if the portfolio grows in value.

Bottom line? If the professional advisor with whom you are working is losing you money, you need to at least get a second opinion. If you aren't getting the kind of return you should be getting, look elsewhere for advice. Human nature is a powerful force. We all appreciate loyalty in other people and we want to be loyal ourselves. That's understandable. In fact, it is an admirable trait. But when it comes to your hard-earned financial resources that you have sacrificed for and done without to accumulate and preserve, business is business. Or at least, it should be. It is disappointing when people stick with "good old George" mainly because George has been their financial guy for so many years they don't have the heart to fire him. The only thing I can tell you, dear reader, is that if you get to retirement age and you're $1,000 a month short, good old George isn't going to send you a check to make up the shortfall.

Changing Times Dictate New Methods

Unless you have been living under a rock for the past 15 years, you know that times have changed when it comes to investing.

During that period of time, who cared what the brokers charged as long as your account was growing like dandelions in the sun? When I entered the financial services industry, I was one of those people who swallowed the pablum fed to us by the big brokerage houses for whom we worked. We were told the stock market was the only place to invest money, regardless of where you were on the financial timeline of life. I used to prepare very elaborate, 140-page financial plans for clients, filled with all kinds of brightly colored pie charts and bar graphs, all to convince the investors of the merits of the stock market over the last 90-plus years.

These fancy documents gave the appearance that we were accommodating their individual needs and risk tolerance. They even projected a specific growth... but it was just that — a projection. There were no guarantees. We had 8 percent plans for conservative folks, 10 percent plans for moderate investors and 12 percent for those inclined to be riskier. I quit doing that just about as quickly as I started when I began to realize that I was sitting across the table from nice people who trusted me with the "rest-of-their-life" money and that the percentages we were projecting were based on nothing more than historical returns.

The more sophisticated I became in my understanding of the dynamics of the market, the more I realized what a bunch of hooey the 8 percent, 10 percent and 12 percent numbers were. At 12 percent, the most aggressive investors would have been projected to have $300,000 for each $100,000 they invested in 2000, when in reality they would have been lucky to have the original $100,000 they started out with. I was so glad I quit doing those hypothetical plans; they would have been a disastrous retirement strategy.

Just because some people in a granite and glass building in the concrete canyons of New York drew a graph 20 years into the future did not mean they knew what was going to happen in the next two decades. No one knew. That became painfully apparent during the decade of the 2000s. Today, to explain away the losses of those crashes and the stagnant market of recent years, there are those who will show you a chart that goes way back in the previous century. They want to factor in these wonderful glory days of the 1980s and 1990s because that raises their projections. All I can say about that is, don't drink the Kool-Aid.

When I retired from corporate America in 1999, I said, "OK, Jeff. What do you do now?" I was in my mid-40s. I was too young for a rocking chair. My hobby was investing, so I took my hobby and turned it into my passion. I had started it when I was 13 years old, and I was still in corporate America during those halcyon trading days of the 1980s and 1990s. I had done pretty well, especially between 1995 and 2000, which were the best years ever for the market. I got out right at the peak of the tech boom, just before the market began its plunge when the tech bubble burst. If I could follow my passion as a career, what could be better? I had garnered enough investing savvy through my personal experience and then through my additional education to become a financial advisor absorbing the education required to officially become a licensed financial advisor, so I took the plunge.

Looking back, I could not have entered the profession at a worse time. The market had just peaked in March 2000 and was poised for a stomach-churning drop. This was a different time, and the market would never be the same. Computer trading had changed Wall Street. The political instability of the world changed the way stocks were traded. Just as a ship has to adjust its sails to accommodate strong winds at sea, I had to adjust my investing philosophies to accommodate the new volatility that now characterized the financial world. To carry the sailing analogy even further, the most useful thing I could do professionally was to help seniors who were approaching retirement find a safer port in which to anchor. When would the next world-shaking event similar to 9/11 take place? No one knew.

Calculating Recovery Time

Something else about time and money dawned on me early on. When people lose money in a stock market account, there is the illusion that if they lose 50 percent, when the market regains 50 percent they have broken even and are back to square one. This is not the case. It was not uncommon to hear of cases where individuals who were approaching retirement lost 50 percent of their life's savings virtually overnight. "Hang in there," their brokers told them. "It will come back." And of course, they were right. The markets did recover. But when you are ready to retire, you are not in a very good position to "hang in there" for the recovery. If you are like most people, you are now in a position where you must begin drawing on your life's savings. Not only that, but the recovery time is often miscalculated. Let me give you an example:

If I have $500,000 in the market and lose 50 percent, I now have $250,000. If the market goes back up 50 percent, how much will I have? Sometimes I will ask that question at my informational seminars. Usually a hand will shoot up with the answer, "$500,000. Then, after a pause, the light bulb will click on over most of the heads in the audience. "$375,000," someone will say. The second answer is correct. The market will have to go back up 100 percent before it gets me back even. This can be devastating if you are retired and need to take money out to live on. Let me introduce you to *reverse* dollar cost averaging!

Coming Back From a Bear Market

You have heard of the bulls and the bears on Wall Street, the two symbols of opposing market forces. The bear is the timeless iconic symbol of a receding market while the charging bull is the symbol of one on an upward roll. Remember, a bear market is commonly defined as a prolonged 20 percent or greater decline in the S&P 500 index. Remember the statistics on bear markets from our earlier introduction to Wall Street? How bear markets come along an average of every 4.8 years? And how the average time to recovery from a bear market is 60 months, or five years.

So let's think about the "break-even period," that's how long it takes for the market to get back to the edge of the cliff from which it descended. It is not necessarily the time it takes for you to regain your lost wealth. Remember, some recessions have been very brief but very deep, like 1987. That little bear market only lasted three months, but the S&P lost a whopping 33.5 percent! The recovery period was about *two years!* What if you had just retired and were now forced to begin withdrawing money from a shrunken account? Those withdrawals would never revive, would they? No. They would be spent.

What about the bear market that lasted from March 2000 to October 2002 when the S&P plunged 49.1 percent and stayed in "correction mode" for 31 months? Many wrecked portfolios from that debacle were never the same again. I personally watched the ticker symbols crawl across the bottom on the screen on Sept. 29, 2008, when the Dow Jones Industrial Average dropped a record 777 points in one afternoon. That bear market officially started in October 2007 and lasted through March 2009 — approximately 18 months — and was the biggest drop since the Great Depression. The S&P lost 56.7 percent. Market recovery time for this one was approximately 5.5 years. Personal recovery? That is a horse of an entirely different color. Many might never recover.

"It's Only a Paper Loss"

I love it when brokers try to console their wounded flock by saying, "Hey, it's only a paper loss. It will come back. It always does." I have one thing to say to that: "OK, if it's just a paper loss, then the gain will only be a paper gain, won't it?" It's not a gain unless you get to *keep the money*. It's not what you make, it's what you get to keep that counts! So if it took us the better part of five years to get back even, that means we are at Oct. 7, 2007, again. We have reached another high in the market. What is it time for?

A healthy economy drives a healthy stock market. Can we call it a healthy economy when millions are still unemployed or underemployed and 47 million are still on food stamps? Can we call it a healthy economy when the Federal Reserve has to prop up Wall Street with a policy of "quantitative easing"? They do this to artificially spur economic growth, but what it boils down to is printing more money to the tune of billions of dollars per day at this writing. How can you have a healthy economy when these issues still exist? Anyone who thinks there is some kind of stairway to heaven in the stock market anytime soon should stay there. But for someone nearing retirement, the best maxim is "slow and steady wins the race." Only gamble in the Wall Street casino with what you are willing to lose.

CHAPTER 7

Where Will My Income Come From?

Young people are bullet-proof and immortal — at least they think they are. And God bless 'em. All their cells are in there multiplying and dividing and they are caught up in the euphoria of youth — and that's just how it should be. Most teenagers are scarcely concerned about where their income is going to come from until they actually land in the job market and have to fend for themselves. *Then* it starts to dawn on them that life is real and full of challenges.

I thought it was interesting that Aegon, one of the world's largest insurance companies, conducted a survey in January and February 2013 titled: "The Changing Face of Retirement: The Young, Pragmatic and Penniless Generation." The title got my attention. Pragmatic and penniless? It sounded like a contradiction to me. If they are pragmatic, wouldn't they be savers and therefore in possession of at least a little stash tucked away for retirement? But the "pragmatic" piece had more to do with the fact that they have faced the reality that retirement is going to be more challenging for them than it was for their parents. The 20-somethings of the

21st century understand the probable stark reality that they will not have pensions, they may not have Social Security — at least not in its present form — and that the stock market is a volatile world that more and more young investors believe is manipulated.

They are called "penniless" by the survey because so many college graduates come out of higher learning with a diploma in one hand and a burdensome student loan in the other. They are instantly saddled with debt and digging out occupies the majority of their earning energy when they begin work and take on family responsibilities. What suffers, of course, is saving. The survey said the average retirement age in 2013 was 63 but will be 67 to 68 in 2050 when these kids retire. The one bright spot in the survey was the indomitable spirit of 20-somethings to save. One-fourth of those polled said they are saving already and half said they would like to begin.

Before I leave this subject, let me say that as a financial educator I am baffled by the lack of financial education in our schools. Where are the classes in high school that would teach kids what compound interest is and how it works? Where are the text books that would give them a working knowledge of the many types of investment and savings accounts? Most young people don't understand the stock market, cash value life insurance, annuities or, for that matter, how to balance a checkbook. Even universities are sadly lacking in such practical education. Young people are prey for credit card companies that wave "buy-now-pay-later" in front of them without educating them one whit about annual percentage rates and the high cost of revolving credit charges. The Aegon survey revealed that many of the young people surveyed would save more if they were presented with "better and more frequent information about their retirement savings." With the billions of dollars we spend on education in this country, it baffles me that most people do not understand how money works and how taxes work. I think it is by design.

Income: No. 1 Concern for Seniors

I don't watch much television, but when I do, I usually skip the commercials if I can. I think most people do, thanks to DVR technology. But a commercial caught my eye the other day that made me look. I don't remember the sponsor, but the gist of the spot had to do with how much money you need to save so you don't run out when you retire. The spot intentionally touches on a sensitive nerve ending for senior citizens, since their No. 1 fear, according to recent surveys, is outliving their income, which translates into losing their independence and likely becoming a burden on their families.

The concept of the commercial was clever. A bearded "professor" walks toward the camera and says, "We asked people, 'How much money do you think you will need when you retire?'" The camera then zooms in on a hand writing the number $1 million dollars on the end of what looks like a large yellow ribbon. The number $500,000 was written on the end of another ribbon. Apparently each ribbon had a different number written on one end. The voice comes back: "We gave each person a ribbon to show how many years that amount might last." They don't show you this, but the ribbons were apparently rolled up and handed to participants in the experiment. You see a large circle marked off in a meadow. One end of the ribbon, the end without the dollar amount, was attached to the center of the circle. The participants were instructed to walk out from the bull's eye of the circle past concentric circles that had been marked off to represent various ages. The next scene shows a woman walking past the camera unrolling her ribbon past the number 65. We don't know how much money was on her ribbon, but the implication is that it was enough to get her past 65. A young man in his 20s guessed enough money to get him to 70. He is shown trying to pull in the ribbon to get it to go farther. The camera then zooms out and you see the circle goes to age 100 and that most people didn't even make it to age 80, which is years before normal life expectancy today.

A middle-aged woman shakes her head, acknowledging her ribbon ran out in her early 70s. "I'm going to have to rethink this thing," she says.

The professor concludes, "It's hard to imagine how much money we will need for a retirement that could last 30 years or more."

The commercial makes a good point. I have had people come to my office in the unenviable position of having so little saved for retirement that I have had to tell them that I honestly could not help them. Sadly, unless they became the beneficiary of some kind of windfall, like winning the lottery or inheriting money from a rich uncle, they would have to either (a) pare down their lifestyle dramatically and/or learn to live on Social Security, or (b) continue to work as long as they were healthy enough to do so. On the other hand, some with whom I have consulted were surprised to learn that, given the amount they had saved, and given their goals, budget, expenses and legacy expectations, they could have retired years ago; they just did not know it. Most people don't plan to fail, they just fail to plan!

The Three-Legged Stool

You may or may not have heard about the three-legged stool of retirement. Whenever I hear that expression, I can't help thinking of the little wooden milking stools I saw as a boy. That was when people actually milked cows by hand. The three legs of the retirement tripod used to be:

- Employer pension
- Personal savings and interest
- Social Security

Why "used to be"? The idea was when you retired, no one leg would get you through retirement comfortably, but with all three of them, you had solid support that would enable you to maintain the same lifestyle in retirement that you enjoyed in your working years. But as we have already discussed, defined benefit pension plans are nearly extinct. That leaves your own personal savings/interest and Social Security to see you through. Some would even argue that those two legs have termite damage. Unless you are the type of person who likes to bury money in the backyard, your personal savings will be placed somewhere. If you place in the stock market, you must be very careful as you approach retirement that you aren't caught in a sudden market freefall like we experienced in 2008 that could wipe out a substantial portion of what you saved. If you place it in a bank because it is safe there, then your nest egg will be protected, but the trade-off — rates of return that are lower than inflation — is unacceptable.

What about Social Security? The skeptics point at alarming national debt and government spending statistics and declare the program could fail you right when you need it most.

Will Social Security Be There for You?

Under current funding, the Social Security Administration expects the program to be able to meet its obligations until 2033. (Some experts believe that year to be 2025). By 2033, the Social Security trust fund will be able to pay only 75 cents of every dollar of scheduled benefits. They have even stated as much on their website, www.ssa.gov, and in Social Security statements. But if you were born prior to the 1970s, that grandfathers you in. Keep in mind, the Social Security program is not a handout, as are some government-run programs. It is a trust to which you contribute with each paycheck. The problem is 10,000 baby boomers are retiring every day. It won't be long before the number of people taking money out of the system will be greater than the number of people putting money into it. According to statistics released by the Social Security Administration, by 2031 there will be almost twice as many older Americans as there were in October 2015 when I wrote this book, upping the number from 37 million to 71 million over that period.

As I write this, lawmakers are at work hammering out a solution to address this imbalance. They could (and probably will) raise the retirement age and delay payouts to younger workers. Congress is going to have to bail out Social Security the same way they bailed out Wall Street, the banks and the automobile manufacturing industry.

When President Franklin Roosevelt signed the Social Security Act on Aug. 14, 1935, the average life expectancy, according to the National Center for Health Statistics, was 61.7 years. FDR probably had no idea that eight decades later Social Security would be such a popular program. If you are running for public office and you merely *hint* that you might tamper with Social Security, you will not only lose the election but you are likely to be tarred, feathered and run out of town on a rail — especially if you are seeking office in an area of the country where the population is mostly senior citizens.

Social Security continues to be effective, but is it enough to live on for most retirees? No. But it is a good foundation on which to build. At least it is guaranteed by the only entity I am aware of capable of printing money — the U.S. federal government. And it is a lifetime stipend — one of the few incomes that are so guaranteed. In defense of our government, when these programs were enacted decades ago, Social Security and Medicare were never designed to sustain tens of thousands of people for five, 10, 20, 30 or even 40 years. Therein lies the problem.

A Savings Shortfall

Let us say the Social Security leg of the stool is solid. That doesn't mean the nation is still not experiencing a retirement crisis. Even before the recession of 2008-2010, people had not saved enough to make up for the loss of traditional pensions. The downturn and slow recovery made things worse. According to an editorial that appeared in the New York Times Sunday Review March 30, 2013, less than half of households ages 55 to 64 have retirement savings. Of those, half have less than $120,000. If they don't have a pension, that leaves Social Security, which pays out an average of $1,265 a month. That's not much above the poverty line.

"Even at higher incomes, up to $57,960, Social Security is the single biggest source, accounting for almost half. Only the top fifth of seniors, with incomes above $57,960, do not rely on Social Security as their largest source of income; most of them are still working," the editorial stated.

Creating Your Own Pension

There is a movement underway in America to create your own pension with the same characteristics as the defined benefit pension plans that were once offered by employers. Necessity in this case has definitely been the mother of invention. Many saw the handwriting on the wall after the 2008 market crash that projections are not guarantees. Projections are somewhat reliable when all is calm economically. They are like tide charts. Dependable to a large degree in predicting high and low tide — *until* an earthquake a thousand miles away produces a tsunami. Then you can throw your tide charts away. They are irrelevant.

After the 2008 market crash, investors — especially the ones who were approaching retirement and saw the decimation of their life's savings through market volatility — began to want guarantees. After two such crashes in one decade, many investors were no longer buying into the idea of "just hang in there." The mood of many began to swing toward guarantees instead of predictions.

Company 401(k) plans allowed workers to save tax deferred and invest tax deferred, but there are no guarantees with 401(k) plans. Who's to say the mutual funds in which most 401(k)s are invested will not suffer losses? For that matter, who's to say that, even if they suffered no losses at all and enjoyed consistent gains, there would be enough in the kitty to continue paying out for the rest of one's life?

There are some who still believe in the 4 percent rule, but they may as well also claim allegiance to the flat earth theory. What is the 4 percent rule? It is an investing formula that calculated how much you could withdraw from a brokerage account in retirement and, if you rebalanced the portfolio each year just right, never run out of money. Let me amend that a bit. You would not run out of money (according to their projections) if you lived to a normal life expectancy. Why doesn't it work anymore? Two reasons, really. Life expectancy keeps creeping up, and the market data on which the formula was based is seriously out of date.

The "4 percent sustainable withdrawal" concept (which is still considered viable by a few Wall Street types out there) was developed in the mid-1990s by three professors from Trinity University in San Antonio, Texas. They tinkered with the math and models of rebalancing the portfolio with a mixture of stocks and bonds and came up with the magic number of 4 percent. It may have worked in the 1990s when the market was on a steady, upward roll. But it just doesn't fly today. As we saw in the previous chapter, if your retirement nest egg is invested in stocks, bonds and mutual funds and you lose 40 percent of your retirement investment savings within a year or two of your retirement, the 4 percent rule will make you penniless fast. If you had retired Jan. 1,

2000, for example, with a portfolio of 55 percent stocks and 45 percent bonds and rebalanced the portfolio each month and increased the withdrawal amount by 3 percent each year for inflation (which is what the 4 percent rule advocates), your portfolio would still have fallen by a third through 2010, says investment firm T. Rowe Price Group. They estimated that your chances of making it through three decades of retirement would be only 29 percent.

So if the government's pension is way short in covering basic needs, the banks are safe but sadly lacking in returns, and the stock market is just too dangerous a place to leave your nest egg, then where can you turn to create your own lifetime income pension plan?

A New Old Solution

I keep my ear close to the ground, looking for trends that point to retirement income concepts and ideas that fit the 21st century, and I have noticed more and more that politicians, economists and financial experts throughout the financial community are taking a closer look at annuities to restore some financial security to retirement income. You hear the word "annuity" more and more in government reports and independent think tanks at universities.

The Wharton School, University of Pennsylvania, is one of the most prestigious business schools in America. Wharton's research in all things pertaining to investment and retirement planning is done by unbiased professors, who have no merchandise to push, no advertisers to please and no agenda to promote. A Wharton paper produced in 2010, titled "Real World Index Annuity Returns," looks deeply into the viability of annuities as an investment and a source of income for retirees. The lead researcher on the project was Professor David Babbel.

It would be easy to dredge up hundreds of endorsements of annuities as the avenue of approach to creating one's own pension for retirement, but difficult to find one as unbiased as Babbel's. I repeat: He earns no commission, salary, gratuity, bonus, compensation or even free pizza for saying that when he retires he intends to put half of his retirement savings into an immediate annuity. The professor is quoted in the Wall Street Journal of May 14, 2011: "I'm going to annuitize enough so that, together with Social Security, I will have enough income to maintain the lifestyle I want."

Today's annuities allow you to get that reliable, sustainable, guaranteed income for life without annuitization — for a fee, of course. Be careful of the many different moving parts, features and benefits. Seek out a retirement planning specialist who is licensed in *both* insurance and securities.

Another unbiased, nonpartisan entity that has recommended annuities is the U.S. Government Accountability Office (GAO). You typically read the GAO's comments as they pertain to reducing wasteful government spending. They also prepared a report titled "Ensuring Income Throughout Retirement Requires Difficult Choices" wherein they listed the two most important choices Americans have to, as the title of the report suggests, "ensure income throughout retirement." They are:

1. Delaying the age when you elect to start receiving Social Security payments; and
2. Converting your cash-balance defined benefit pension into a lifetime income annuity rather than taking a lump-sum payment upon retirement.

The report is clear in its recommendation that middle-class retirees should convert at least half of their retirement savings into a lifetime income annuity. According to the GAO report, a majority of people with defined benefit retirement plans choose to annuitize at least a portion of their retirement cash balances rather than take a lump sum. This could be the most important decision in one's life and should not be made without guidance from the right advisor.

Many of today's annuities offer a lifetime income stream without annuitization!

CHAPTER 8

Is It Time to Rethink Annuities?

Just as an experiment, I will sometimes ask a classroom or an audience what they think of an investment that I will describe in detail but give a pseudonym. For example, I will call it something like "guaranteed lifetime investment vehicle," or something jazzy like that. Then I proceed to list on a whiteboard all the characteristics of this investment as follows:

- Guarantee of principal
- Goes up when the market goes up
- Stays even when the market goes down
- Capable of producing guaranteed lifetime income
- Always maintain control of account
- Limited liquidity for 10 years but full liquidity after that
- Tax-deferred growth
- Unused portion of account passes to heirs upon death

Then I ask them to vote. Those who like the sound of this investment and would like to know more, raise your hands. Nearly every hand goes up. Now, those who do not like this and are not at all interested, please raise your hands. Usually, no hands go up.

Next I ask how many here like annuities. Usually only one-fourth of the hands go up, and those are people who own them and have had satisfactory results. Of course, most present are surprised to learn that the "wonder investment" I just drew on the board is a fixed index annuity with an income rider attached.

I can't help but think of William Shakespeare's famous and often misquoted line from Romeo and Juliet: "What's in a name? That which we call a rose by any other name would smell as sweet."

So why the bias? Why is it that when you say the word "annuity," some people make the sign of the cross with two wooden pencils as if Dracula had just entered the room? Like most prejudice and bias, it has its roots in misinformation and a lack of education, which are two things people who know me well know I just cannot abide. The cure for misinformation and ignorance is, of course, information and knowledge.

What Is an Annuity?

The word "annuity" comes from the Latin "annu" or "annus," which simply means "yearly." In ancient Rome, soldiers were given an annuity, or an annual salary, when they retired from the military. The idea has carried on in various forms since then. British businessmen developed life expectancy tables in the 16th century and came up with contracts that would allow private individuals to create their own annuities, or lifetime yearly payments. The arrangement was that a contract holder, or annuitant, would pay a lump premium to an insurance company in return for a yearly stipend later on in life. That basic idea of annuities has evolved into various financial instruments, which perform all manner of functions along the same basic theme. We also get our English words "annual" and "anniversary" from the Latin root for year. There is nothing frightening about that, is there? Good so far?

Nowadays, an annuity is a contract purchased by an individual from an insurance company. An annuity is an investment vehicle that is usually used to secure retirement income and pays a fixed number of payments over a set time period. That's a broad-brush description. Naturally, every insurance company will have different provisions and terms, but that is the basic concept. You might say that an annuity is a genus within the family of insurance products and there are several species within that genus. The term automobile may include Fords, Chevrolets, Toyotas, etc. Those makes come in different models, such as convertibles, sedans, pickup trucks and SUVs. Not all annuities are created equal, and to think that one name fits all is as silly as assuming that all automobiles are the same. The five basic kinds of annuities are:

- Variable
- Immediate
- Fixed
- Index
- Hybrid

Variable Annuities

When people come after you with a pitchfork when they hear you say the word "annuity," they are probably thinking of a *variable* annuity. Why? *Because variable annuities can lose value.* They are essentially stock market investments in an insurance wrapper, inside of which you have subaccounts, which are essentially mutual funds that contain hundreds of stocks. They go up in value when the stocks go up. When those stocks fall, your account value falls. With variable annuities, for example, you can start out with $100,000, and a month later, have only $80,000 in your account... or less, depending on how your stocks perform. During the stock market crash of 2008, many who had variable annuities experienced this.

Why bother with the insurance wrapper? Why not just buy mutual funds? Because they contain certain provisions that only insurance companies offer. For example, a death benefit can protect the investment for heirs. Let's say you lost half of the value in your variable annuity because you or your advisor picked the wrong fund. The death benefit would ensure that the heirs receive the original principal. Just to be clear, let's assume that you have a variable annuity that was once worth $100,000 but is now worth $80,000. And let's say that you have a $100,000 death benefit. How much can you withdraw from your variable annuity? Only $80,000, less any remaining surrender charges. You cannot withdraw the $100,000 death benefit. Just because variable annuities have death benefit options doesn't mean they are protected from market loss.

As with any other annuity, gains accrue tax-deferred and taxes are paid when those gains are withdrawn. Because variable annuities have subaccounts similar to mutual funds, they also come with expenses and fees that fixed annuities do not have. These charges may include mortality fees, administration fees, income rider fees, expense risk fees, 12b-1 fees and extra charges for the optional death benefit. Fees, fees, fees! They can average 3 to 4 percent! You should see the look on people's faces when I expose to them all the fees they are paying in their variable annuities!

Immediate Annuities

With an immediate annuity, you may choose to begin receiving a payout right away — thus the term. It is immediate, as opposed to one you pay into over many years. The immediate annuity payout can vary according to several options that are available. The payout can run for a certain length of time. This is known as "period certain." The payout can extend for the rest of your life. What about the amount paid out? That will be determined by the insurance company using life expectancy tables. The payout can be set up so that it comes to you every month, or every year for the rest of your life and/or your spouse's life if it is set up as a joint annuity.

With a lifetime payout, using the figure $100,000 for easy math, a 67-year-old male, for example, can expect to be paid $577 per month for the rest of his life. Even if he lives to be 102, the payments will continue. That's the good news. With a traditional immediate annuity single life only payout, you get the higher payout; however, if you die a year after opting for a payout, the insurance company keeps the balance of the account and the heirs get nothing.

This works the same as most pensions. I have had people come into my office and say they have annuities when what they actually have is a pension. With pensions, when you die, that huge pot of money that you built stays in the pension fund for others to use. None of it goes to your heirs.

You can have an immediate annuity with a five-, 10-, 15- or 20-year payout. You can even have a refund immediate annuity. You get the highest payout if you take a lifetime immediate annuity, which is the one that pays you a certain sum of money while you are alive, and when you die the contract is over and heirs get <u>nothing</u>.

To illustrate, let's say you are a 67-year-old male and you put $500,000 into an immediate annuity. Your payout may be $34,608 per year, every single year, for as long as you live, or $2,884 per month. The same $500,000 for a 65-year-old female would yield an annual payout of $30,348 per year for the rest of her life, or $2,529 per month. Why is it lower? Because, generally speaking, females live longer than males. So when calculating a lifetime payout, the insurance company takes into consideration your age, sex, how much you deposit and the payout option.

Fixed Annuities

A fixed annuity is a little like a bank CD, only with an insurance company. Let's say you put in $100,000 and, five years from now, if you're earning, say, 3 percent in interest, you will have $115,927.40. There is one significant difference between a fixed annuity and a CD. With a CD, you pay taxes as you go. Even if you leave the gains with the CD, you still pay taxes on the gains. Fixed annuities, however, are tax-deferred. They usually come with a slightly higher rate of return than a CD. Rates can go up and down just like a CD.

Like CDs, you will pay a penalty if you withdraw money from a fixed annuity before the surrender period expires. This penalty is called a "surrender charge." With fixed annuities, surrender charge periods are usually between three and seven years. Once the annuity is past the surrender charge, you can withdraw your principal and any gains penalty free. You will pay taxes at the time of the withdrawal on the gains. You may roll it over into another annuity without paying taxes by using a 1035 exchange, or leave it in the same contract. As with any annuity, the owner may "annuitize," or exchange the balance of the contract for a payout that can either last for a certain number of years or may be guaranteed for the life of the annuitant.

A more popular option in the last 10 years is to opt for an income rider instead of annuitizing. Why? Because if you annuitize and die early, the insurance company keeps the balance of the account. With an income rider, the annuitant still gets a lifetime payout and, should he or she die early, the balance of the accumulation account is passed on to heirs.

Index Annuities

Index annuities are sometimes called fixed index annuities (FI-As). They were once called equity index annuities, but that term is seldom used these days. The index annuity is a type of fixed annuity that provides a minimum rate of interest, just like the traditional fixed annuity. It is sometimes called a "floor." With these annuities, the rate of return over that floor is predicated on the performance of a stock market index — usually the Standard & Poor's 500 (S&P 500) index — thus the name, index annuities. In recent years, some companies offer indexing based on the S&P 500, the DOW, the Nasdaq, the Euro or a blend of several indexes. There is one now which offers a blend of the S&P 500 and the TVI Index, which is a blend of commodities.

The insurance company sets a cap ranging 3–9 percent on this feature, which means that you get a portion of the positive returns of the market, but do not participate in any of the downsides. In other words, if your cap is 8 percent and the S&P jumps 20 percent in one year, your growth will hit your 8 percent cap and stop. The caps are a tradeoff for having a guarantee of principal. If the index loses 20 percent, the value of the index annuity is not negatively affected. In that year, you get a zero rate of return. In a case like that, however *"zero* is your *hero,"* because eliminating the negatives enhances overall growth.

Different companies have different rules, percentages and structures. Some have participation rates; some do not. Fixed index annuities are relatively new, having come along in the 1990s. They have become increasingly popular with seniors and baby boomers approaching retirement because of their growth potential combined with safety.

The moving parts of this annuity have been described as a "ratchet/reset" mechanism. At the contract's anniversary date, the growth is locked in and becomes the new high-water mark of the annuity. That amount now becomes the new balance and represents the new amount that cannot be lost due to market fluctuation. These annuities grow tax-deferred and can be annuitized, or converted into income streams of various lengths or a lifetime income stream. The addition of income riders has made annuitizing less attractive, however.

Depending on the insurance company offering it, index annuities can come with a bonus. Insurance companies compete with brokerage houses, banks and other insurance companies for your money, and bonuses are offered to attract customers. The insurance company adds a bonus to the amount you deposit, and this is included in your account balance. If the insurance company offers, say, a bonus of 7 percent, and you deposit $100,000, your account value is immediately $107,000. The catch is that you are committing to a period of time, and although the bonus is added to your account value on day one, most bonus annuities have a vesting schedule.

Hybrid Annuity

A hybrid annuity is merely an index annuity with an income rider attached. It is sometimes called an "income annuity." For example, if you put $500,000 into a hybrid annuity, and the insurance company pays a bonus of 8 percent, you're starting off with $540,000. That is the *income* account value. That same $540,000 is also going to be what is referred to as an "income base." In essence, with a hybrid annuity, you have two accounts running simultaneously. The historical average rate of return for an index annuity over time is somewhere in the neighborhood of 6 percent. But let's assume worst case scenario and say that the actual account value grew by only the 1.25 percent guarantee. After 10 years, you would have an account balance of at least $611,426.

Simultaneously, as the *actual* accumulation account is growing, the $540,000 *income base* or *income account* grows as well, rolling up at, let's say, 7 percent per year. This percentage of growth varies from company to company, but the idea is the same. If you had $540,000 to work with, for example, that income base rolls up at 7 percent per year. So at the end of 10 years, in the income base account, your $500,000 is now $1,062,262. If, at that point, you want to turn on that income rider, you may do so.

What you receive in the way of income is based on your age. If you are 75, for example, you would typically have a lifetime payout of 6.5 percent, or $69,047 per year. The income would come every year (or every month, if you wish) for the rest of your life. To extrapolate that, let's say you get $69,047 per year for 20 years. You would collect $1,380,940 when all is said and done, even though you only put in $500,000.

And what happens if you die sooner? Let's say a tragic accident occurs and both you and your spouse are killed after having collected only three annual payments from your lifetime income — you would have collected a total of $207,141. Your *actual* account value (not your *income* account) at that time would have grown at only the 1.25 percent guaranteed rate and would be $634,642. So when you subtract what you have taken from the real account value, there's $427,501 left for the heirs. Why is that important? Because in an immediate annuity you put the money in, and you get a payout for your life, but once you die, it's done; your heirs didn't get any money. With the income rider, you get the best of both worlds. You get a guaranteed income that you can't outlive, and if you pass away, your heirs get the difference between the actual account value and the amount of income you took.

If you are looking for income you cannot outlive, the hybrid annuity is probably the best solution. They are not for everyone, and they are by no means a one-size-fits-all solution to every income planning problem. But they have some exciting features.

By using the hybrid annuity as an income source, you may be able to delay taking your Social Security until age 70, which will make that income as high as possible. You may also have an income that will keep up with inflation and be greater than it would have been had you taken it at age 62, and you reduce your taxes.

I would be less than forthright if I told you that a hybrid annuity did not come with a few moving parts. It does. And no one should buy any annuity without understanding all the parts and how they work. If your financial advisor cannot answer your questions to your complete satisfaction so you know the features and benefits of the annuity, you are working with the wrong advisor. The biggest confusion I see with the hybrid annuity is between the income account, which has no cash value, and the actual cash value or death benefit. I still run into many people who believe that an insurance company adds 7 percent to their actual account balance every year, regardless of market performance! That is wrong, wrong, wrong! It goes back to what I always say at my workshops. Do not invest in anything you don't understand.

Fees and Commissions

Contrary to statements made by those who are not acquainted with fixed annuities and fixed index annuities, they come with no charges and no fees except for optional riders. The hybrid annuity, for example, charges a fee of usually 1 percent or less per year of the contract value for the lifetime income rider. Brokers and those who typically offer variable annuities do charge fees called loads, since they are typically invested in mutual fund type investments. If you buy a variable annuity, you will pay these fees, as well as the broker or banker's commissions, even if you lose a portion of your principal. By contrast, fixed and fixed index annuities have no risk, no fees except for the nominal charge for optional riders, and no commissions that come out of your balance. Any commissions paid to agents are paid by the insurance carriers that produce the product, similar to the way an airline pays a travel agent. It doesn't come out of your pocket; it is built into the product. Your fee is the time and use of your money. Know how much you are paying in fees!

Growing in Popularity

One way to tell if a restaurant has good food is to look at how many cars are in the parking lot at lunchtime. In the last few years, fixed index annuities and hybrid annuities have been growing in popularity at an astounding rate. There is good reason for it. When Professor Babbel of the Wharton School ran his numbers in the 2010 research presentation paper titled "Real World Index Annuity Returns," he found that, based on data from 15 FIA issuers, FIAs outperformed conventional investments during much of the 10 years measured. According to Babbel's report, from 1997 through 2007, the five-year annualized returns for FIAs averaged 5.79 percent, compared to 5.39 percent for taxable bond funds and 4.73 percent for fixed annuities. From April 1995 through 2009, FIAs beat the S&P 500 over 67 percent of the time and beat a 50/50 mix of one-year Treasury bills and the S&P 500 79 percent of the time. During eight five-year periods starting in 1997 through 2004, their data shows the FIAs they looked at offered an average annualized return ranging from 4.19 percent to 9.19 percent, with no negative years. By contrast, an investor in the S&P 500 would have seen four positive five-year periods and four negative ones. The year the Wharton report came out saw FIA sales soar to $8.2 billion in the second quarter, up 22 percent from the first quarter, as investors looked for an alternative to volatile equities and low-yielding bonds.

The main reason many of my clients are in fixed index annuities with income riders (hybrid annuities), however, is not because of the cash value so much as it is the feature that provides a guaranteed income for the rest of their lives. They are, in effect, taking charge of their own retirement by forging their own private pension. They know that their money is going to grow and compound. They know that they can use the guaranteed income feature and still pass on any unused portion to their spouse or heirs. This is a far cry from the old style of annuity, where you received an annuity payment but surrendered control of the balance of your account so that, when you died, the insurance company kept the money.

This Is Not Grandma Ruby's Annuity

My Grandma Ruby was born in 1900 and grew up in Colorado. When she was a young woman, she came to Portland via covered wagon. She never had more than an eighth-grade education. She worked as a clerk at Meier & Frank Department Store in downtown Portland for 45 years and retired in 1965. These were the days when corporations provided pensions for loyal employees, and Grandma Ruby's pension would have guaranteed her $8,000 per year for the rest of her life, or she could take a lump sum of $100,000. Grandma Ruby had no formal education, but she was intelligent. She had heard from a fellow retiree that there was something out there called an annuity. She had also heard that if she

Before You Sign ...
Do you have a pension coming upon your retirement? Do you have an option to take a lump sum? Before you decide on either, sit down and talk with a financial advisor and learn what your options are. You may be able to parlay that offer into a much better payout and provide an enduring legacy for your spouse and heirs. Once you make your decision, however, it's made and there are no do-overs. Before you sign anything that you can't take back, take the time to know your options. The key question to ask when it comes to your retirement income is ... is it guaranteed?

took the lump sum offered to her from the department store and parked it with an insurance company, they may be able to offer her a better deal. Ruby opted to take her lump sum and buy a single premium immediate annuity with a life-only payout of $832 per month, or just short of $10,000 per year for the rest of her life. It was a sweet deal for Grandma Ruby. Female life expectancy in 1965 was 70 to 72 years old. She lived to be 98 years old. As it turns out, it was be the single best financial decision she ever made.

I remember Grandma Ruby for many things. I am convinced she was the best cook west of the Mississippi. She made fried chicken in a black cast-iron skillet that would have made Colonel Sanders' mouth water. She served it with gravy and mashed potatoes that were the best I have ever tasted. But the first time I ever heard the word "annuity" was when my grandmother would occasionally mention it. If she had a purchase she wanted to make that was over and above her usual expenses, she would say, "I'll wait until my annuity check comes."

It would be years later that I would learn all about the inner workings of annuities and how the moving parts of them function. In her day, there were few options. Grandma Ruby could have received a greater monthly amount from the insurance company had she opted for a five-year or a 10-year payout. She had no way of knowing she would live to be almost 100 years old. But regardless of which option she chose, once she "annuitized," or opted for a guaranteed payout of any length of time, she no longer controlled the balance of the account. Had she died accidentally six months after purchasing her annuity, there would have been no death benefit for her heirs.

That's the way single premium immediate annuities worked in those days. But the old style annuities aren't "flying off the shelves," so to speak. The baby boomers just weren't too keen on the use-it-or-lose it idea. The insurance companies re-tooled and came out with the modern hybrid annuities that (a) allow for a guaranteed income like Grandma Ruby had, but without sacrificing control of the account, and (b) predicate gains not on a fixed rate of interest but on the upward movement of the stock market.

As in life, misconceptions can warp our judgment when it comes to investing. Back in the late 1980s, there was a television commercial that used the catchphrase "this isn't your father's Oldsmobile." Oldsmobile had come out with a sporty Cutlass Supreme model. It was a very attractive car with lots of power, class and style. But, for some reason, it wasn't moving off the sales lots. The reason was that the perception of the Oldsmobile was that of a stodgy, gas guzzling, old person's car. General Motors wanted to let the world know that this new Oldsmobile was a departure from the old one. To re-establish the brand's identity and appeal to a younger audience, the automaker aired thousands of 15-second spots with visual images of young people putting the perky new Cutlass through its paces. Each clip ended with the voice-over, "This is not your father's Oldsmobile."

These new-style annuities, with their multi-faceted options and high-horsepower earning capabilities, are not your grandma's annuity by any stretch, which is why we need to rethink them as viable instruments for retirement income planning. For most people, they lay a foundation for the portion of their retirement nest egg that must be safe, reliable and sustainable income for life.

CHAPTER 9

Building Your Successful Retirement House

April 5, 1972, started out as a beautiful spring day in Vancouver, Washington. But, as the day wore on, a squall line of thunderstorms began rolling northeast across northern Oregon. Big trouble was brewing in the form of an F3 tornado that would kill six people, leave more than 300 injured and do as much as $6 million in property damage.

Students watched the storm develop through the windows of their classrooms at Fort Vancouver High School. They saw a cloud as black as a bruise form, and the day suddenly went dark. "It was as if someone turned the lights off outside," one student said. They could feel the air pressure change, and suddenly hail the size of golf balls began pelting the windows. This was followed by a deafening roar as the twister formed and touched down. The high school kids watched in horror as nearby Peter S. Ogden Elementary School was hit. The tornado lifted the roof off the building. Walls collapsed and then the roof was slammed back down. It was as if the twister was picking its targets. The high school was untouched, but the elementary school was demolished.

Without thinking, students and teachers ran across the field that separated the two schools to render assistance. They heard the screams and moans of the little kids trapped under debris and began pulling them out. Seventy students were injured but miraculously none were killed. St. Joseph Community Hospital would soon be packed with frightened and crying children, worried parents and scurrying doctors and nurses.

The storm would also demolish a grocery store and several homes along its nine-mile path of destruction. The tornado struck a bowling alley, killing a woman. Five shoppers would die in the grocery store. It would go down in history as the deadliest tornado ever to hit the area. As this is written in 2015, it still holds that infamous record.

Interestingly, you can drive through the neighborhoods that were hit by that tornado and it's as if nothing had ever happened. It appears that all the homes have been rebuilt from their original foundations. In some cases, wood-frame houses were turned into splinters and shards, but beneath each of them was a concrete slab enabling the house to be rebuilt better than it was before.

Importance of a Financial Foundation

In many respects, the foundation is the most important element of any building. When you stop and think about it, it's what everything else rests on. If the foundation isn't properly laid, the rest of the house may not function in its intended role. A well-constructed house is an apt metaphor for a good financial plan. We begin with a stable foundation of *safety* — CDs, savings, annuities, pensions and Social Security. We can count on them to be there no matter what the market does or doesn't do. The returns of these wellsprings of money are both predictable and reliable. As of this writing, interest rates on CDs, savings accounts and money market accounts are at an all-time low, paying somewhere between zero and 1 percent.

When we put that in place first, then our fiscal house can withstand anything, even the whirlwind losses some experienced in the stock market crash of 2008 when the market dropped nearly 50 percent. Just as it makes no sense to decorate the walls of a house before the foundation is in place, it is foolish to "gamble" in the market with money we can't afford to lose There is the time-honored "rule of 100" to consider. Personally, I view it more as an investing guideline to accommodate risk than a rule, but it helps us gauge how thick our foundation should be. It goes like this: Take your age and subtract it from 100. The amount you subtracted is the percentage of your assets you should have completely safe, altogether free from market risk. Another way to figure it is by putting a percent sign after your age. That is the percentage of your money that you may have, and often should have, safe and guaranteed.

Let's say you are retired and in your 70s and you are thinking about how much of your assets you should have at risk in the market. The above guideline would help you achieve that balance. But the same should apply if you are in your 20s or 30s. If you are 25 years old, you should be saving toward retirement and putting around 75 percent of your money at risk where there is a greater possibility of long-term reward. Why not? Time is on your side, and there is no reason you shouldn't take full advantage of the risk/reward element of the stock market. Most young people don't realize that if pensions and Social Security may or may not be there for them, they may be retiring on just one leg of the three-legged investment stool — their own personal savings and investments. My observation is that most young people don't follow the rule of 100, choosing to waste their money on cars, gadgets and expensive toys instead of investing it.

The same lack of fiscal symmetry is true of many retirees and pre-retirees as well. Far too much of their savings could be swept away by the next big market crash because far too much of it is at risk. Then they are vulnerable to what I call the "catch up" syndrome. That's when they lose a chunk of their retirement savings, take a glance at their retirement timeline and say, "Oh no! I must make up this loss right away!" That's when they go Las Vegas, shoving all their chips on the line hoping for a big win, which rarely pans out. They are no longer in their accumulation years. This is a time for them to be cautious with their assets because the next market downturn could catch them by surprise and the risk they took could produce unfavorable results, indeed.

The Bible says Jesus was a carpenter. So I guess he specialized in finish work. But being in the trades, he must have had a good knowledge of how the rest of the house should be constructed to come up with the following illustration:

"Therefore, everyone who hears these sayings of mine and does them will be like a discreet man who built his house on the rock. And the rain poured down and the floods came and the winds blew and lashed against that house, but it did not cave in, for it had been founded on the rock. Furthermore, everyone hearing these sayings of mine and not doing them will be like a foolish man who built his house on the sand. And the rain poured down and the floods came and the winds blew and struck against that house, and it caved in, and its collapse was great." — Matthew 7:24-27 (New World Translation)

Truer words were never spoken, as my mother used to say.

The Walls

With the foundation in place, now we can build the walls of our financial house. You need a strong roof, which we will get to in a moment. When I think of properly constructed walls, I can't help but think about a big stink that occurred a few years ago in

Florida during the housing boom. It seems that either contractors couldn't get enough building materials or they were trying to shave a few dollars off their cost, but they began using what later became known as "Chinese drywall." It was a type of drywall that was made in China and imported to the United States beginning in 2001. The first sign something was wrong was when new homeowners began noticing a "rotten-egg" odor permeating the house. Apparently the stuff was made with a corrosive material containing high sulfur content, and a big class-action lawsuit resulted.

When constructing our walls, we want to make them out of sturdy materials that won't crumble or ruin our financial house. I call these our *alternative investments.* Some are not publicly traded. Some go public and we have the potential to see large capital gains in higher percentages.

As this book is written in October 2015, banks have tightened lending criteria. But companies seeking to grow find alternative ways to raise capital and one of them is through a financial instrument known as a real estate investment trust (REIT). I have always loved real estate but I have never owned a rental house. Several of my clients have made a lot of money in real estate as landlords, and one reason they are successful is because they have the right temperament for it. Personally, I confess that I would not make a good landlord. I call the reasons I am not interested in becoming a landlord "the three T's" — toilets, tenants and trash. I am just not well suited for any investment that I have to clean, repair or paint. I also despise the idea of having to go through that awkward business of collecting money from tardy rent payers. Too many headaches. But by being part of publicly traded REITs, you essentially own real estate all over the country and someone else cares for all the tedium that goes with property ownership.

This segment of the economy runs in cycles. As I am writing this in the third quarter of 2015, it is not a good time to sell residential real estate, but it is a good time to buy it. I like REITs because you can invest in the types of real estate that are attractive at the time, such as buildings designed with an aging population in mind — medical and dental offices, hospitals, assisted living facilities and the like. Who are my tenants? Folks with high credit ratings, doctors and dentists. They also like to sign long-term leases with built-in step-ups in rent each year. With these, we get a check every month and our clients can either take that and use it for living expenses or reinvest and buy more shares at a discounted price.

With this section of your financial house, it is important to understand the risks. These are, after all, securities — the part of the financial house that is not guaranteed but is solid. Remember what happened in the Enron collapse? When that corporation went under, there were people in line to be paid from the bankruptcy liquidation. The first to be paid was Uncle Sam. Then who? That's right! The landlord in the form of those companies who owned the real estate investment trusts. Guess how much was left after the rent was paid and Uncle Sam got his money? *Nothing!* Nothing for the stockholders and bondholders. They were at the bottom of the list and lost everything.

The Roof

The roof is last. Whenever a storm blows in and brings wind and hail, the roof is the part of the house that suffers the most damage. It is just like that with our financial house. The roof is where we will install our high-risk, high-reward assets. Yes, they will be the first to take a hit, but they will also be the first to have the biggest gain from the market. The roof of your financial house will represent the riskiest holdings in your portfolio because they are exposed to things that we cannot control. The list of uncontrollable things includes such things as natural disasters, terrorist attacks and any other unexpected event that can impact the way the market behaves. This is where we put traditional investments like stocks, bonds, mutual funds, 401(k)s, oil and gas, variable annuities and managed money.

The roof of your financial house can be replaced if damaged. These investments that carry more risk represent the portion of your assets that, according to the rule of 100, you may place at risk because of the potential for a greater reward. A key point to remember is that you only do that *after* your lifetime income and other non-market investments are in place to balance out the risk.

Uniquely Yours

Once completed, your fiscal house should be one in which you can move around comfortably. It needs to fit your lifestyle. Think of how personal your residence is to you. From the pictures on the walls to the articles in the pantry, it reflects your choices, your taste, your preferences. Likewise, your financial house should be custom-built to your specifications. You are not likely to be satisfied with a pre-fabricated house, one that is manufactured in a warehouse and then trucked to a lot and set up on blocks. You need the careful attention to detail that only a skilled and caring architect can provide.

For example, how much do you need in the way of guarantees for the foundation? I mentioned one kind of alternative investment for the walls, but there are several. A skilled financial advisor will ask lots of questions and seek your input before designing your plan. For example, I know one couple with assets to live much more lavishly. They could live in a larger home, drive more expensive cars and dine at fancy restaurants. But they don't. They lead a modest lifestyle and live very frugally because they both feel strongly in passing on a legacy to their two children and three grandchildren. Here's where having a financial architect comes in.

In this case, both the husband and wife were in good health. They were pleasantly surprised to see how they could use life insurance as a legacy tool. Since the goal was to pass along as much of their accumulated wealth to their children as possible, they took out a second-to-die life insurance policy (used frequently in estate planning) to make their children the beneficiaries after the last surviving mate passes away. The couple wished to leave $1 million to their heirs. Since insurance companies only charge between 5 percent and 10 percent of that amount to provide a $1 million face amount, it made sense to transfer the burden to the insurance provider. Oh! Did I mention that the proceeds of the life policy would be completely *tax free?* The husband and wife team were owners of a successful business. They had worked hard to grow their enterprise and keep it going for three decades. They were also intelligent and well educated. But this simple strategy had simply not occurred to them. It was not in their "wheelhouse," as the expression goes. Now that this couple had their legacy provisions in place, they could enjoy some of their hard-earned money with a clear conscience and a sense of peace. The one thing I couldn't do was teach them how to relax and enjoy themselves. The last I heard, however, they were in the process of figuring that out on their own.

Your financial house needs a designer and a builder. Hire a professional to help you construct it. You may be pleasantly surprised at how much more comfort and security the right planning professional can add to the layout of your financial house. If you hire the wrong person to construct the most important house of your life, the results could be disastrous.

CHAPTER 10

Health Care - The Scary Subject

For most Americans, health care is indeed a scary subject, especially if you don't have a plan for it. Deanna Pogorelc is a Cleveland-based reporter who writes about health care. In an article in Med City News dated Aug. 22, 2013, she showed just how much the cost of medical treatment has increased in the United States by displaying an actual hospital bill from 1965, compared to a hospital bill dated Aug. 21, 2013. In both cases, the patient did not have health insurance, so the charges on the bill were due and payable upon receipt of the services.

In the 1965 bill from a New Jersey hospital where a woman gave birth, the line-item description of services were shown next to the cost for each[5]:

Four days in a hospital room - $19.00 per day. Total $76.00
Nursery care four days - $5.00 per day. Total $20.00
Laboratory - $21.00
Drugs and medicine - $14.10

---

[5] Deanna Pogorelc. MedCity News. Aug. 22, 2013. "Fastest Way to Feel Depressed and Angry About U.S. Healthcare? Read Medical Bills on Reddit." http://medcitynews.com/2013/08/just-how-expensive-is-healthcare-in-the-u-s-these-hospital-bills-posted-on-reddit-say-it-all.

Delivery room - $20.00

Medical and surgical supplies - $2.00

Television - $2.00

Total charges - $165.10

Contrast that bill with one received by a woman Pogorelc describes as an "uninsured patent who went to the emergency room with stomach pains." She was given morphine and several tests and then released six hours later. Her bill was as follows:

Emergency department - $3,308.00

Pharmacy - $92.95

Ultrasound - $1,003.00

Pathology/Lab service - $469.00

CT scan - $ 6,867.50

Radiology - $445.00

Central supply - $246.00

Total charges - $12,431.45

Shocking, isn't it? I get the impression that today's medical bills are bloated with waste and blatant profiteering and rife with redundancy in the name of "care" to inflate the bill. It is a national shame and politicians seem to either skirt the issue when cornered with hard questions about health care, or come up with elaborate programs that don't work. As this is written in 2015, the Affordable Care Act, colloquially known as "Obamacare," has been launched but so far shows no sign of fixing the problem. It remains a scary proposition, indeed!

I hope I'm not bursting anyone's bubble when I tell you this, but there is no such thing as free health care. Somebody has to pay for it. The problem with health care is that everyone wants someone else to pay. I wonder who picked up the tab on the $12,431 run up by the woman who went to the emergency room with stomach pains. A lot of times, it's the hospital. They write off what is uncollectable. But those charges don't just disappear. They show up in higher costs of everything the insured patients use in the way of hospital care.

Some of my senior clients are just ordinary folks. If they have one major health event and end up in the hospital for, say, three weeks, and then are forced to go from the hospital to an assisted living facility for a few months of extended rehabilitation, it could wipe them out financially. The average cost of assisted living facilities in Vancouver, Washington, where I work and live, is $4,250 per month. According to "A Place for Mom," a senior care referral service based in Seattle, there are 30 assisted living facilities within nine miles of Vancouver.

Government programs like Medicare and Social Security were never designed to sustain health care for millions of people for 10, 20 or 30 years. These programs are like two-lane roads that were built in the 1930s to accommodate a tenth of the traffic they must carry today. I'm afraid that the nation's young people — your children and grandchildren — are going to end up footing the bill from the costs incurred by this generation and the deficits that have resulted.

Sometimes when I am speaking before a group on the subject of our financial future, I like to poll the audience. "How many think taxes will be lower in the future?" No hands. "How many think taxes will be higher in the future?" Every hand goes up.

That's the right answer. In Chapter 2 of this book, we did the math on the apparent national indebtedness and the true level of indebtedness if we figured in Medicare and Social Security obligations. And the math simply does not lie. So higher taxes it will be.

Who would have imagined years ago that medical science would have advanced to the point where it is today? We have expensive wonder drugs and huge diagnostic machines that use the latest in technology. We can get new hips, new knees and transplanted organs. It seems that not a day goes by that I don't hear of a client or friend who is in the hospital having some new part put in. But at what cost, and borne by whom? As I write this in October 2015, Medicare pays for most of it for those over age 65. With 37 million seniors in this country and the baby boom generation boosting those numbers at a daily rate, it makes us look again at the simple math of the situation. I am in the middle of the baby boom generation — those born between 1946 and 1964. There are an estimated 84 million of us, and we are getting older every day. On average, 10,000 baby boomers turn 65 every day, a social phenomenon that will continue for years to come. Eventually, we are going to need some of those replacement parts. Who is going to pick up the tab for them?

The Sandwich Generation

There is a new term I hear and read about a lot these days: "The Sandwich Generation." No, it is not referring to the generation whose diet now consists largely of sandwiches from McDonald's and Wendy's restaurants. This is a social phenomenon that was rarely observed before the 1990s — Americans who are near retirement age and find themselves caring for aging parents and "boomerang" children (those who return home after a fractured marriage or some other personal failure). As if it was not difficult enough to care for their own needs, these retiring adults are now sandwiched between two obligations that, whether real or perceived, are met at their own expense, both personal and financial. So much for their dreams of a carefree retirement spent listening to the ocean waves under swaying palm trees.

The Pew Research Center says that one of every eight Americans aged 40 to 60 is caring for a parent while raising a child. The sandwich generation is growing in numbers for several reasons. People are living longer, the population of people over the age of 85 is increasing in number, and few are prepared for the expense of long-term care.

That last one is the real culprit. People just don't want to think of what will happen to them if they become too sick or feeble to take care of themselves. So they postpone making decisions about it. Estimates are that less than 10 percent of American seniors have any type of long-term care insurance. If you ask an insurance agent to explain a traditional LTC policy, it sounds like he or she is speaking a foreign language. You have elimination periods, daily benefits, limitations and exceptions and all kinds of other terms that even many insurance professionals have a difficult time understanding, let alone explaining them to prospective policy buyers.

Another reason why it is human nature to bury our heads in the sand when it comes to long-term care insurance is because the cost blows us away. The best time to buy traditional LTC is, of course, when we are younger and have no health concerns. The longer you wait, the more expensive it is, and if you have health problems that would point to your needing the care, you probably won't qualify for the insurance. The insurance companies are in it for profit. None of them want to "buy a claim."

Situations vary from person to person and are affected by geography. But an individual who is age 60, for example, might pay $200 per month for a policy that provides $150 per day for a maximum of three years. Don't forget, traditional LTC insurance is a use-it-or-lose-it situation. If you pay all of that money for decades and then "die with your boots on," so to speak — and never have to enter a long-term care facility or receive home health care — all of that money is down the tubes. Meanwhile, you are living life, making mortgage payments, buying cars, sending the kids to college. It's easy to see why so few have taken the insurance companies up on their offer for LTC coverage and wind up either becoming a ward of the state or a burden on their children.

An Alternative Approach

Did I just make the point that insurance companies are in business to make a profit? You can easily deduce that just by looking at all the skyscrapers they own and the expensive commercials they air on television. They also pay attention to the buying patterns and general disposition of the American public to their product offerings. A few years ago, when they saw this stampede of retirees coming along, they saw both problems and opportunities:

- Millions of Americans would need long-term care of some description.
- They would not have the resources to pay the high cost of it on their own.
- Their traditional long-term care policy offerings with the old use-it-or-lose-it approach weren't very popular.

Denizens of the free enterprise system that they are, the insurance companies did what automobile manufacturers do when their cars aren't selling. They retooled. They didn't get rid of traditional long-term care insurance. You can still buy it if you wish. But they introduced coverage in different packaging. In the early 2000s, the actuaries and statisticians got together and came up with some innovative approaches to solve the problem. These new solutions were designed to attract customers without breaking the bank. One way was to attach LTC options to annuities and life insurance policies. In the insurance industry, these are combination policies are known as "hybrids."

Hybrids

The name "hybrid" is an apt one because it represents two financial products rolled into one. In one of the most popular of this new breed, the first piece may be a fixed annuity that provides a minimum return, typically of around 3 percent per year — nothing great, but better than a CD — with a long-term care policy built in. The best part about this arrangement is that if the funds you invest are never needed for long-term care, the combo acts just like any other fixed annuity. It can sit there and grow, just like a CD with an insurance company instead of a bank, only tax deferred. You can turn it into an income stream at some point in time, choosing either a guaranteed lifetime income or income for a certain period of time. Or you can leave it alone and pass the asset on to heirs. But if you do need skilled nursing care, assisted living or home health care, the amount you put in comes out first with most of these types of policies. The benefit is triggered by your need for the care, and then the policy will, in essence, provide as much as three times the amount of the annuity balance. Most of the people I have interviewed would prefer to be cared for in the comfort and convenience of their own home. Wouldn't it be nice to have someone care for you in your own home and get tax-free leveraged money to pay for it?

Let's say, for example, you purchased a $100,000 annuity/LTC combo with a selected benefit limit of 300 percent and a two-year long-term care benefit factor. After you spend the $100,000 you put in, then you have an additional $200,000 available to pay for the care. So the annuity you purchased for $100,000 could potentially pay out three times that in LTC benefits. That's just a middle-of-the-road example. Some are more generous than others and there are offsetting trade-offs and available options.

When these first came out, I went through the wording of the policy looking for "gotchas." Frankly, it looked too good to be true. I finally put my magnifying glass down and had to admit that it was a pretty darn good replacement for the unattractive traditional LTC policies out there. There is a degree of underwriting, so you may not qualify if you are seriously ill. But that varies. Some companies are more liberal with their underwriting guidelines than others. Some companies require a physical examination by a paramedic and others just go on medical records. No, you won't get rich off the 3 percent interest (or whatever it happens to be at the time), but compared to bank CDs, it isn't too bad. Also, you have to put the money in all at once for it to work. It is also a plus that, under the Pension Protection Act of 2006, a provision that became effective on Jan. 1, 2010, LTC benefits may be paid from an annuity, tax-free.

Life Insurance/LTC Hybrids

The annuity/LTC hybrid may be just right for someone who in good health, age 60 or over, and has the cash to invest. The life/LTC combo may be the solution for those who are in relatively good health and under the age of 60. Why? Because the older you get, the more you pay for life insurance of any description. The life/LTC policies are typically bought with a single premium, just like the annuity combo. The premium is usually around one-third to one-half of the death benefit (face amount). The long-term care benefit is usually around 2 percent of the death benefit per month. For example, if someone bought one of these combination policies and paid a $50,000 premium into a $100,000 life policy, the cash value (not the surrender value) would be in the neighborhood of $50,000. But the LTC benefit would be somewhere in the neighborhood of $2,000 per month if it was needed. You need to know that whatever money is paid out in LTC benefits reduces the policy's cash value by the same amount and with these, a physical exam is usually required.

These are just a couple of the more popular alternative approaches to LTC coverage that are available these days. They have a few moving parts, so make sure you understand how they work before you obligate any funds and make sure you are dealing with an insurance professional who isn't just selling policies but has a fiduciary responsibility to you. That having been said, the hybrid plans are definitely making acquiring LTC protection less scary.

Long-Term Care Isn't Cheap

Assisted living costs vary depending on several factors, which typically include:

- Geographic location
- Size of accommodations
- Level of care required
- Additional amenity and service fees

This shouldn't surprise us. The cost of real estate varies by geographic area, and so does the price of medical care in general.

Just as the cost of real estate varies by geographic area, assisted living costs also vary nationwide. According to the 2012 "Market Survey of Long-Term Care Costs" conducted by the Metropolitan Life Insurance Company (MetLife), the national average for assisted living base rates was $3,550 per month in 2012. You can count on that going up, it seems. According to the 2013 "Cost of Care Survey" conducted by Genworth Financial, assisted living showed the largest rate increase since 2012 among all categories of senior care, rising 4.55 percent. Residents of assisted living communities can typically expect a 3 to 5 percent annual increase in their base rate. In the states of Washington and Oregon, a one-bedroom, single-occupancy assisted living apartment will cost monthly:

Oregon: $2,309 minimum, $4,023 median and $6,570 maximum.

Washington: $1,075 minimum, $4,250 median and $7,500 maximum.

Some think nursing home cost is covered by Medicare, but they are thinking about short-term care. The limit on that is typically 60 days, and even then, it has to be preceded by a qualifying hospital stay. Nursing home care provided from this point on is typically considered long-term care, and patients must rely on other types of insurance coverage or pay privately. The only other alternative is to spend down their assets to the point they qualify for Medicaid, which is a state-administered program for low-income folks. In other words, they must officially become a pauper.

Again, nursing home costs vary depending on geographic location and whether a patient receives care in a private or semi-private room. According to the 2012 "MetLife Market Survey of Long-Term Care Costs," the nationwide average daily rate for care provided in a private room was $222 and, in a semi-private room, $248. Here is the breakdown in the average per-day nursing home rate for Oregon and Washington:

Oregon: $235 semi-private, $256 private room.

Washington: $251, semi-private, $280 private room.

Medicaid, the health insurance program for low-income people, pays for about 70 percent of all nursing home patients. Options are more limited for patients on Medicaid than for those who are paying their way, either through insurance benefits or from their own funds. Anything the government gives you will have myriad rules and strings attached. Suffice it to say that once you go the route of spending down your assets to qualify for Medicaid in an attempt to protect your own assets, it is not easily done. There is a five-year look-back period on assets. Any attempt to place your assets in the names of other family members will be carefully scrutinized. My recommendation is to consult with an elder care attorney to make sure of your footing. Your choices are clear. Buy some form of LTC insurance or be self-insured and risk spending down your assets until you have to go get in line with all the other people who went this route. I don't think the latter will be a line you will want to be in.

Resources Are Available

If you find yourself confronting some of these health care decisions, it can be intimidating. But the Internet is a useful tool and there are lots of organizations out there that are willing to help you. They won't tap you on the shoulder, however. Some of these organizations are government-sponsored, some are nonprofit and others are commercial. Some of the programs are national with local chapters to give you individual, person-to-person assistance. All you have to do is Google the subject you are interested in and then use good judgment in which you select. Just for grins, I typed the words "sandwich generation" into my search engine and came up with almost a million sites. I discovered that there is even a Sandwich Generation Month. So if you thought you were alone in the world, you're not. I can't list everything available to you in this book, but I know of a few helpful resources. The website www.eldercare.gov can be of invaluable assistance to you in dealing with aging parents. Operated under the auspices of the U.S. Administration on Aging, the website is a treasure trove of resources. Also, check out the National Council on Aging (NCOA) at www.ncoa.org and, if it involves Medicare or Medicaid services, www.cms.gov. Look into www.govbenefits.gov to determine if they may be eligible for government benefits.

CHAPTER 11

Keep One Eye Open for Inflation

I started driving in 1970. My first car was a 1956 blue and white Ford sedan, a color selection we called a "two-tone" in those days. My kids don't believe me when I tell them that in 1970 we paid a quarter for a gallon of gas. I could fill up the 20-gallon tank for $5, but I usually didn't. The drill went this way: Drive up to the pumps and remain in the car. There was no need to get out. The attendants inside the gasoline station were alerted to our pulling onto the lot by a "ding" that sounded when our tires ran over a pressurized rubber hose. When the bell rang twice, two men came out. One raised the hood to check the oil and the other came to the driver's side window and asked, "Fill 'er up — regular or ethyl?" To which I would usually reply with "two dollars' worth."

Even more incredible to my progeny is the fact that, for the few cents of profit they made on the transaction, these men would wash the windshield and check the air pressure in my tires. More often than not, the last thing I saw as I drove off was a big smile and a friendly wave.

In 1970, the average cost of a new home was $38,000. My wife, Brenda, and I built our first home and moved into it on her 21st birthday. It had a lawn, paved driveway and everything else that went with it, including a mortgage of $41,000. That was a lot of money back then. My mother thought I was crazy. "Jeff, how do you ever expect to make those $240 monthly payments?" she asked, shaking her head.

These days, a new house that size would cost more than $250,000. That's inflation. Just think about the prices of things today versus what they cost in 1970. Postage stamps, a loaf of bread, a candy bar, a movie ticket.

Many remember the late 1970s and the early 1980s when inflation raged like a forest fire. During the Jimmy Carter administration, inflation jumped from 9.4 percent in 1974 to 14.7 percent in 1980. People who saved money at banks during those days had the illusion of good times. Sure, their CDs and money market accounts grew by double-digits, but they were paying twice as much for groceries and gas as they had been five years before. Those who had to borrow money in order to buy a car or a house found they could not afford the payments. So they didn't buy. The building boom stopped dead in its tracks in 1979 and entire subdivisions of homes that builders had constructed on speculation remained vacant for years. Ironically, as things turned out, the cure for hyperinflation was the recession that the inflation had spawned. Like a sailing vessel with a heavy keel, the economy will usually right itself if left alone.

As of this writing in 2015, the inflation rate hovers around 3 percent or less. While the inflation of the 1970s and 1980s was like a raging river, the inflation of the last few decades is like a slow moving stream. The erosion is barely perceptible unless viewed over time, but it is nonetheless there.

Will hyperinflation like that ever return? Who knows? There are some doomsayers who warn of a return to double-digit inflation in the near future through skyrocketing oil prices. But their fears are mostly speculation. What we do know is that steady inflation at 3 percent per year is almost a given and, unless you are prepared for it, can be a financial death by a thousand cuts. In 2014, the government gave a whopping 1.5 percent cost-of-living increase to Social Security recipients.

When it comes to income planning, failure to plan for inflation is the same as planning to fail. To demonstrate how much inflation pinches the retiree, consider the effect inflation would have on income requirements in three different scenarios. Just to make the math easy, let's say you needed to supplement your Social Security by $1,000 per month. How big would your nest egg have to be, earning 7 percent in interest, if you lived 20 years in retirement? How about if you lived 30 years in retirement? Now figure in 3 percent inflation. How does that affect the picture?

Impact of Inflation on Income Requirements

Most people don't realize that these small cost-of-living increases in Social Security benefits and government pensions are **not** keeping up with inflation. If you live 20 years in retirement, you need $129,734 to produce $1,000 monthly income — no inflation!

- If you live 20 years in retirement, you need $163,007 to produce $1,000 monthly income — 3 percent inflation!
- If you live 30 years in retirement, you need $195,343 to produce $1,000 monthly income — 3 percent inflation!

Look at a dollar like it's a little worker for you. Every time you spend it, you're firing it. It can no longer work for you. My father, whose name was Raymond Dixson, was a hard-working man who knew the value of a dollar. This is mainly because he had to work two and sometimes three jobs to support a family of eight while I was growing up. He would never begrudge me some small luxury with which I would indulge myself when I was growing up if it was my own money. I had a paper route when I was nine years old. But he would say, "Son, you can either have the money, or you can have what the money can buy — but you can't have both." In other words, once you spend it, that dollar is gone. You can go out and earn another one, but that dollar (and the opportunity to save and invest it) is gone forever.

Meaning of Money

As a financial professional, I try my best to first find out what people want out of life and then figure out the best way to put their money to work to that end. In other words, I want to know what their money means to them. It does mean different things to different people. When you stop and think about it, money is merely numbers on paper until you attach a purpose to it. That's one reason why I believe the way we keep score is not so much by the rate of return as the materialization of your hopes, dreams, desires and the vision for the future you hold.

As mentioned earlier in this book, the decade of the 2000s was referred to as the lost decade (and the jury is still out on the one that followed it) because advances were negated by declines. That is why, even though there may be a place for stocks, bonds and mutual funds in a balanced portfolio, I believe that a steady, upward, reasonable rate of return is much more important to your investing success when you are in it for the long haul. Slow and steady, in other words, wins the race. That is especially true when you consider that most people in the last decade or so were lucky if they merely broke even in the stock market. When you factor in taxes and inflation, most came out on the losing end.

When you are thinking about the 3 percent inflation erosion of your money, think not just in terms of numbers, but what those numbers represent — the erosion of hopes and dreams, visions and goals, and, most of all, the erosion of the guarantees of independence in later years. Any financial plan that does not allow for at least 3 percent in inflation needs to be rethought. We don't know what inflation will do any more than we know what the news headlines in tomorrow's newspaper will be. Most of my clients agree that the cost of living and taxes are going up, not down. While we hope for the best, we plan for the worst just to be on the safe side.

CHAPTER 12

The 21st Century Retirement Challenge

We have talked about a lot of things in this book. The way I look at it, the top six retirement concerns for the 21st century boil down to these, not necessarily in any particular order:

1. Government spending
2. Taxes
3. Inflation
4. Market volatility
5. Living longer
6. Health care costs

I call it the 21st Century Retirement Challenge because, when we retire, we are going to be impacted by these six things, to one degree or another. In order to meet the challenge, we must devise a workable plan and then keep alert to changes that can occur that may necessitate our making changes. The people I see fail at this are those who become mentally lazy and stop paying attention. Or they let someone else handle their financial affairs and did not stay on top of things. You just can't do that, not in the fast-paced world in which we live today. You have to keep your eye on the ball.

When I think of keeping up with all we must do these days just to keep pace, I am reminded of something I haven't seen in years, but yet made a big impression on me as a kid. On Sunday evenings, our family used to gather in front of our small black-and-white TV and watch "The Ed Sullivan Show." In those days, the variety show was a favorite for prime-time television entertainment, and Ed Sullivan was a master at it. The man was a consummate showman but he could neither sing nor dance, told lousy jokes and couldn't play a note on a musical instrument. His gift was finding people he knew would entertain a mass audience and bring them to his stage. It was Ed Sullivan who introduced the Beatles to America in 1964 and started Beatlemania over here.

You could always count on the show having a juggling act or two, a guy riding a unicycle across a high wire, singers, dancers and animal acts. But quite possibly one of the most famous and skilled multitaskers that ever graced his stage was an Austrian fellow by the name of Erich Brenn — better known as "the plate spinner." He was a regular. His thing was to start spinning plates on flexible poles, one at a time, and keep them all going until he had as many as 15 spinning at once. One would get wobbly on the end and he would hurry over to get it spinning again. The tension would build when, while he was attending to one wobbler, another one would lose its spin and almost fall only to have him save it in the nick of time.

Do you ever feel like that guy spinning plates? We have so many hats we wear, especially if we are family people. When it comes your time to retire, life doesn't stop. You swap one set of cares and concerns for another. Job one now is to keep the gears of this new station in life functioning smoothly. Keep this retirement machine operating, and work out the bugs as they appear. Maintain the centrifugal force, if you will, of all the spinning plates — income, expenses, budget, taxes. Your multitasking no longer pertains to your old job, but now you have frequent decisions you must make regarding what has now become a largely nonrenewable resource. You must keep it working for you on one end while depleting it on the other end.

You Need the Right Kind of Help

This may sound self-serving, as my chosen profession happens to be this line of work, but that makes the fact no less true — you need help to get it right. To win the retirement game, you need a coach — the right coach. You just do.

A competent, experienced financial retirement coach can help clients know what moves to make and when to make them so they can keep all your "plates" in motion. How to save, invest and grow your money. How to tackle your specific financial goals. How to deal with contingencies, such as helping a family member out in times of need without endangering your own financial security. Should I pay off the mortgage? In what circumstances should I consider a reverse mortgage? Am I paying more than my fair share of taxes? Is my estate in order? How often should I review my will? How do I know if I need a trust? Those are just a few of an entire range of financial matters on which you could err in judgment without a coach — errors that could seriously jeopardize you financially.

Whatever you do, don't confuse financial planners with stock brokers. Many stock brokers have about as much interest in your total financial well-being as the person who sold you your last automobile. The answer to every question you pose to a stockbroker will end up being a ticker symbol, not a strategy for building, maintaining and utilizing wealth to a purposeful end. One of my favorite sayings goes like this: "If all you have is a hammer, everything begins to look like a nail." People may call themselves financial advisors on their business cards and on their office door, but if they only deal in securities, they will likely offer the same suggestion for every problem you present to them.

Anyone can hang out a shingle as a financial planner, but that doesn't make that person an expert. They may tack on an alphabet soup of letters after their names, but that doesn't mean they are a fiduciary, one who is legally bound to put your interests ahead of their own.

Don't be afraid to ask how your financial candidate gets paid. It's not a personal question; it's business. You don't want a conflict of interests from the person you hire to give you advice. You want unbiased opinions from a professional who operates independently and is not tethered to any one particular company or set of financial products. Those folks are salespeople. There are no cookie-cutter solutions in today's complex world for a person seeking financial peace of mind in retirement. Nobody works for free, so make sure you know exactly how much you are paying in fees associated with your investment.

Why Can't I Just Do It Myself?

This is America. Sure, you can do it yourself. But you really don't want to go it alone when it comes to managing your money, any more than you would want to perform self-surgery to remove your own appendix or become your own dentist. For most, it's not worth the time and ongoing effort required to manage your own investments. In addition, as you get older, busier and, hopefully, wealthier, your financial goals become more complex and your options change.

Every January, I make it a point to go through the stacks of periodicals and bulletins I have accumulated from the previous year. I file what I need to keep and toss out what has become obsolete. The sands of the financial landscape are constantly shifting. Keeping current with it requires 20 percent of my time, just reading, studying and scanning for changes that affect the financial well-being of my clients. My point is that what you don't know *can* hurt you when it comes to managing your financial affairs in retirement.

The Game Plan

At Northwest Financial & Tax Solutions, Inc., the basic X's and O's of our game plan boil down to this. We will attempt to:
1. Reduce risk.
2. Reduce fees.
3. Reduce taxes.
4. Give our clients a reasonable rate of return.
5. Educate our clients so they can make good financial decisions.

Reduce Risk – Many of our clients have told us over the years that before coming to us, they didn't know there were any other places to put their money besides the banks and the stock markets. Don't get me wrong. I believe the stock market is sometimes an appropriate place for some of our clients' money, but not always. Why? Because, to engage in a bit of understatement, the market is subject to a lot of volatility. That may be exciting and even prudent for a young investor to be involved with, but for those who are in retirement or ready to retire, it can be a financial disaster. When it comes to the market, we prefer to engage in active money strategies versus the old passive money strategies, such as buy and hold.

Reduce Fees – Our pledge is to always be transparent. No one works for free. We inform those with whom we work about any fees they are being charged in connection with their investments placed in our care. We believe in intellectual transparency. You need to know the "why" of your investments. Why do I have my money here, and what are the reasons for this strategy over another one? It is our responsibility to seek out investments that make the most sense for our clients.

Reduce Taxes – It is our belief that you should not be paying taxes on money you are not currently using. Most of our clients don't mind paying their fair share of taxes; they just don't want to pay *more* than their fair share. We look for ways to legally and ethically reduce taxes. There are many tax-advantaged, tax-deferred or even tax-free investment options available.

Reasonable Rate of Return – When it comes to determining what a reasonable rate of return is for the portion of your portfolio that is at work for you, that number needs to be one that can, at a minimum, beat the current inflation rate. You have likely heard that if you want to beat inflation over time you must have a diversified portfolio of stocks, bonds and mutual funds. These are only some of the choices you have today when building your financial house. Most people have not been exposed to the other asset classes that have no correlation to the stock market. There are many more options out there, which could be better for your specific situation. It is our belief that to generate retirement income, you must have enough money making money, so you don't have to go back to work for a paycheck. It may not be enough to use a pile of money until it's gone.

Education – We believe in educating our clients. Whoever you select as your financial advisor should be willing to educate you about the finer details of your investments. We believe it is necessary for clients to know where every dollar of their portfolio is invested, why it's there, what fees they are paying and how it is expected to perform. It is critical that they understand the tax advantages or disadvantages of any investment. It is essential for clients to know the annualized rate of return for each of their investments and, more importantly, their exit strategy.

Our aim is to design a customized and comprehensive portfolio based on each individual client's needs, not force them into a plan that isn't the right plan for them. The three-step process should be:

- **Discovery.** We just talk and get to know each other to see if we are a fit. Sometimes we are not a good fit for each other, and it's best to know that up front.
- **Evaluation and education.** In order to get to where you are going, you must first know where you are. This is where we evaluate your present position financially and identify the strategies that could get you to where you want to be.
- **Identify and explore your options.** This usually takes place in the third meeting when we thoroughly review all options available to you and, if appropriate, implement a plan of action.

Knowledge Is Not Necessarily Power

There is an old fable about a miser who used to hide his gold at the foot of a tree in his garden. Every week or so, he would go and dig it up and look at it just to feel good. One day, a robber noticed this and went and dug up the gold and ran off with it. When the miser next came to gloat over his golden treasure, he found nothing but the empty hole. He wailed and moaned, tore his hair and cried so long and loud that all the neighbors came around. He told them how he used to come and visit his gold.

"Did you ever take any of it out?" asked one of them.

"No, I only came to look at it," replied the miser.

"Then come again and look at the hole," said a neighbor; "it will do you just as much good."

I love that story, because it makes the point that knowledge can be as precious as gold. But if you don't apply it, it is worthless. I sincerely hope that some of the things you have learned from my book will make a positive difference in your life and help you win the game of retirement. That will only happen if you put what you have learned to action. Just as wealth unused might as well not exist, knowledge if not acted upon is useless.

It reminds me of the old story about the difference between *knowledge, understanding* and *wisdom.*

Knowledge is the accumulation of facts. If you are standing on the railroad tracks, for instance, it is a fact that you know you are standing on the tracks. If the train is coming, you know that, too. You possess the knowledge of what a train is and that it is approaching.

Understanding is when you comprehend the relationship between things. You are aware of the fact that the train is made of hard, inanimate steel and you understand that the impact of that steel with your soft tissue would be fatal.

Wisdom is getting off the tracks.

ABOUT THE AUTHOR

Jeff Dixson is not only the founder of Northwest Financial & Tax Solutions, Inc., but the company's heart and soul. NWFTS reflects Jeff's convictions about what true financial success is and his passion to help people achieve it.

Growing Up

Jeff grew up poor in a large Catholic family with four boys and three girls. His father was a postal worker, who usually worked two or three jobs because he had so many mouths to feed. "Our family was all about togetherness," says Jeff with a laugh. "We lived in a very small house. My three brothers and I all slept in the same room. I didn't get my first pair of new shoes until I was 9 years old when I started my first job delivering newspapers. The shoes were required for the job. They were a business necessity. I used to get up at 5 every morning and go to work before going to school."

Jeff says he doesn't regret his humble beginnings because it helps him relate to people from virtually any background. He describes his father, Raymond Dixson, as an honest and industrious man and his mother, Aida, as someone who was well loved by all who knew her and was regarded as a loyal employee. She worked full-time until she was age 75.

"She was a hard-working woman of Italian descent who always put her family first and had more friends than anyone I ever knew," Jeff says, adding that his father taught him to have a sense of humor and to take pride in whatever job he did.

Corporate America

Jeff spent many years in corporate America working for one of the largest grocery store chains in the country. He started out as a courtesy clerk and went into management at age 17. By 19, he was the grocery manager, and at 21 he was given the keys to a $10 million per year supermarket and was charged with the management of more than 100 employees. From there, he kept moving up the corporate ladder to become a store director, grocery sales manager and the youngest district manager in the company's history. As grocery sales manager, he had charge of purchasing for 41 stores. He also set prices, did shelf placement and wrote all the weekly ads.

"Corporate America started to sour with me into my 40s," says Jeff. "At that point, I knew it had provided a great lifestyle for me and my family, but it just wasn't fun anymore." Jeff walked away from the six-figure income, great benefits and five weeks' paid vacation. "It was just time for me to do something different," he says.

A New Direction

"I had always loved investing," Jeff remembers. "It was a hobby of mine, so I began to think of turning it into a profession." He spent a significant time studying to become a financial advisor and started his new career in March 2000. He eventually opened up his first office in an Exec-U-Suite building where he had little more than a desk and a telephone. After he was there for a year and began to develop a small following of clients, he moved into what he likes to call his "little engine that could" office.

"It was a start," Jeff recalls. "The office was so small that it reminded me of the little house where I grew up. It had a gravel parking lot and an old wooden ramp that creaked as you walked up it. My wife was embarrassed to even come by. We had one room that measured 12 by 16 feet, and, somehow, we crammed four desks in that one little space. There was also a small conference room for my office. But we grew too fast and our roster of satisfied clients soon forced us to move to larger quarters."

The Best Ideas Are Drawn on Napkins

Jeff built his brick-and-mortar office building that today houses Northwest Financial & Tax Solutions, Inc. from a sketch he drew on a napkin while flying home from a business trip to San Diego. "I wanted our clients to love coming here, and I think they do." Jeff says. "The comfortable 'lodgey' feel is like no other financial services office and really makes people feel at home."

The Formative Crash

Jeff's view on investments was shaped by something that happened right after he decided to leave his corporate job.

"The stock market crashed in 2001, shortly after I left the corporate world and began outlining my new career," says Jeff. "I lost more than $1 million in personal assets. Fortunately, it was not everything we had. Much of my money was tied up in the stock of the company I had been with for decades, and the share value dropped from $67 per share to $20 per share in six months and never recovered."

Jeff says that he realized at that point if he was going to enter into a profession that had at its center helping people with their hard-earned wealth and life's savings, he had to have a game plan that would make winners and not losers out of his clients.

"I did not blame anyone but myself for the losses I sustained in the stock market crash, but I was bound and determined that the game plan I would develop would first preserve and protect wealth and then build and sustain it."

That process became the pillars of his financial services company and is still the blueprint used by the three advisors and support staff of 12 who work at Northwest Financial & Tax Solutions, Inc. today.

Family Life

Jeff met his wife, Brenda, when he was 15. He describes her as his "first and only true love."

"Our younger brothers were teammates on the same Little League all-star baseball team," explains Jeff, "and we got to know each other attending the games."

Jeff and Brenda married in 1975 and are parents of three adult children: Jeromy, Brent and Brianne. They also have seven grandchildren: Parker, Tyler, Avery, Luke, Blake, Addison and Harper.

"I have been so blessed," says Jeff. "Over the years, I've sat knee to knee with thousands of people. I have heard their stories. I've seen people with tears running down their cheeks, some in pain and others in joy. All of that has touched me and shaped my business."

Jeff admits that helping other people is what fuels him. "I get up each and every day with one thing in mind: to help as many people as I can," he says.

ACKNOWLEDGEMENTS

No project such as this would be possible without the support of family, friends and coworkers. I must say thank you to some people without whose help I could not have written this book: First and foremost, my family. I want to thank my wife, Brenda, who has given her support and helped me in so many ways that they are impossible to count. I thank my three children, Jeromy, Brent and Brianne, for inspiring me to be the best I can be at anything I have ever sought to accomplish. My seven grandchildren, Parker, Tyler, Luke, Avery, Blake, Addison and Harper, are the future generation Americans who are destined for greatness. I thank them for their inspiration and wish them Godspeed.

Professionally, I would like to thank Bud Abraham, my first coach in grade school at St. Stephens School in Portland, who coached multiple sports and always had winning teams. He taught me that in order to win in any game, including the game of life, you must be disciplined, committed, focused and willing to work harder and smarter than your competition. He taught me the fundamentals of success.

To my best friend and mentor, Gary Imel from Gig Harbor, Washington, for unselfishly giving of himself to help me reach my goals and for teaching me to dream BIG! His leadership and professional approach is unmatched in the financial services industry. Never have I met a man with a bigger heart.

Finally, I wish to express my sincere appreciation to all members of my incredible team at Northwest Financial & Tax Solutions, Inc., who have helped make our company one of the top independent firms in America.

Jeff Dixson offers securities through Madison Avenue Securities LLC (MAS), member FINRA/SIPC. Jason Lambert, David Topper and Dustin Martin offer securities and advisory services through MAS. MAS and Northwest Financial & Tax Solutions, Inc. are not affiliated companies.